MIRRORS OF LIFE

Part 2

The Fight for Political Power

by Neal Owens

Copyright 2020 by Cornelius Owens

All rights reserved. No part of this book may be reproduced in any form or by any electronic or mechanical means, including information storage and retrieval systems, without written permission from the author. The only exception is by a reviewer, who may quote short excerpts in his/her review.

This book is a work of fiction. Names, characters, places, and incidents are either products of the author's imagination or used fictitiously. Any resemblance to actual persons, living or dead, or locales is entirely coincidental.

Cover Design by Rick Taubold

Published by Owens LLC

www.owenspublishing.com

Facebook – neal.owens.733

Instagram – owenspublishing

Twitter – @CorneliusNealO1

ISBN (Paperback): 978-1-7331503-3-0

ISBN (E-book): 978-1-7331503-4-7

Dedicated to my wife and best friend, Brenda, and our twenty years of marriage.

Special Thanks to all the readers of this novel.

CHAPTER 1

All eyes were locked on Derrick as he stared into his mother's sanpaku eyes. The only sound was from the television seemingly unheard.

Six seconds passed, and he reluctantly said, "Welcome to the team."

Yvonne tilted her head to the side with the smile in her eyes. "Thank you. Now, what is my role?"

"Role?" Derrick leaned forward with both palms cupped on his knees. "Ma, what role do you want?"

"Human Resources and Community Liaison."

He leaned back with his hands locked at the back of his head. *She knows I oversee human resources. She's taking the load off my plate. But community liaison will put her on the front line. She will become a target, and she knows it.*

Derrick shifted his eyes to the others at the table: Juna had worry written on her face; Charlene and Amari had blank expressions; Xavier and Gladys appeared poised.

He leaned forward with his hands clasped between his knees. "Ma, you know community liaison will make you a target?"

She stared with protective eyes as the others were locked in silence. Two seconds that seemed like five passed before she said, "I know. I told you that they will have to kill me to kill you."

He considered that before he said, "You got it." He slapped his knees, stood, and sauntered toward the bedroom.

"Where you going?" Juna asked.

To hide his watering eyes, he didn't turn around and kept walking. "To get my phone."

He entered the bedroom, grabbed his phone off the night table, and stepped onto the bedroom terrace.

His eyes lifted toward the sky as if he was trying to see the throne of God. He marveled at the full moon in the daylight. *What does it mean?* He pondered that for several seconds before he voice-activated one of his playlists, and the tune by Sonnee became another question in his troubled mind.

He turned on his phone, looked across the Manhattan skyline, and he saw a beautiful world covered by the ugliness of its inhabitants.

The group at the kitchen table was trying to calm Juna's uneasiness when Derrick ran in, cell phone raised in his left hand, and yelled, "Ryan left a message!"

They scuttled around him as he sat on the black Belgian linen U-shaped sectional sofa and anxiously played the message on speaker.

"Hi, Derrick. I called earlier but didn't leave a message. Arthur sent me the address of my wife and children. I'm outside their home now, but I'm afraid to knock on the door. Just calling to get your advice. Talk to you later."

Derrick shouted, "Did you hear that? It proves that Ryan didn't commit murder-suicide. I need to give this message to the police."

Gladys said, "Not yet. As your mother stated earlier, let them fall into the pit they dug for you."

With his enthusiasm lowered, he said, "Elaborate?"

Gladys leaned forward with her arms on her knees. "The police will question you today or tomorrow. When they come, mention the conversation you had with Ryan about Arthur. The police will interview him, and I'm sure he will say that he didn't find any information on the whereabouts of Ryan's wife and children because I don't believe he knows that Ryan left you a message."

"Okay, that will solidify Arthur as a suspect, but it's not a crime to lie to the police. So why not turn it over now? The police won't mention the message until after they have questioned him."

"It's not a crime to lie to the police," Gladys said, "but it is a crime to lie to the FBI. Your film company is still is under their investigation, and Ryan was the CFO—so they will coordinate with the police investigation and expedite their own.

"After you meet with the police, schedule an interview with the FBI and let them hear the message. They will ask if you shared the information with the police. Tell them that you just discovered it. The FBI will take possession and question Arthur, and he will tell them the same story that he told the police. Then they will know there is a conspiracy and indict Arthur that he might lead them to the others."

Charlene interjected, "Smart play."

Gladys continued, "But transfer all of your contacts and files before you give them the phone."

Yvonne rolled her head to face Derrick. "You see how God works. If you weren't in church, you would've gone with Ryan."

She was right. He sighed and looked at his mother, in need of her guidance.

Yvonne read his eyes. "God saved you again. This time because you were in church. God is telling you that it's time for you to start going to church on a regular basis."

He narrowed his eyes, pursed his lips, and angled his head.

"Derrick, I know how you feel about church, but these are demons that prayer and fasting can't cast out. Two kids were shot in the back of the head."

Charlene said, "Ma, how do you know they were shot in the back of the head?"

"Because I read the underground news alert."

"The underground news? You can't trust that."

"Yes, you can. NPR reports the uncensored news." She gave her daughter a stern look. "Who would execute children? These are wild beasts that are more powerful than the FBI."

"If they got that much power, how can we stop them?" Charlene asked.

"They don't have more power than the wisdom that is in us from God. I have a plan."

"A plan? What is your plan?" Derrick asked.

Yvonne stood. "The election and reelection of the black president is proof that we can elect another black president, or Hispanic, or Asian, or Indian. America has become a diverse country. The racists are no longer the majority. But they still hold political and financial power.

"We are gaining financial power and will continue to gain if we harness our political power. That requires us to motivate people to vote—not only for president, but Congress and state and local legislatures. The largest group of registered voters are independents. We need to target that group with inspirational candidates that are progressive and moderate."

"Where do we find the candidates?" Derrick asked.

"That will be my job."

Gladys said, "I get the feeling that you already have some in mind."

Yvonne shifted her eyes. "I do."

"For your plan to work," Xavier said in his baritone voice, "we have to motivate people to vote in all the elections. Only half of the eligible voters go to the polls in the presidential elections, and that is the largest turnout. What's your plan to motivate people to vote?"

"Teens are the future voters," Yvonne said. "I plan to focus on them before they become eligible to vote. Initiate their interest in voting by making it feel cool to vote. Advertise young voters waiting in long lines to vote as a social outing—taking selfies, meeting new friends, having a pizza party. Put DJs outside the voting precincts where a large number of eligible young voters reside. Identify young candidates to run for the school board and city council. Young candidates attract young voters. Inspirational candidates create enthusiasm. Those are some of my ideas."

"Those are very good ideas, but I don't trust politicians," Derrick said. "They say what you want to hear but go with the wind."

"True. That's why we have to vet the candidates we back. That is my job."

"Ma, that is a big job and very expensive. I can't commit my money to that project."

"I'm not asking for your money. But I need in-kind donations from your film company to make and advertise commercials on your platforms."

"How is that not asking for money?"

"You know the difference. Besides, you need political strength to empower black communities. You need political strength to prevent future projects from being blocked. You need political strength to ensure sustainability."

His eyes reflected the realization.

Yvonne shifted her eyes across the group. "We cannot make an impact on this year's presidential election, but we need to be ready for the midterm. The racists are afraid of losing their stronghold, so they are working while others are sleeping. Derrick, all of your work will be in vain if the racists maintain political power. I told you that before."

Derrick's tongue was twisting side to side in his closed mouth. His eyes ran across the others before returning to his mother. "Everything you mentioned is on point. But I can't spare the money you need for a nationwide project. That's why I didn't follow up."

"Okay. Tell me, how will you sustain your investments? Do you think all you need is money? Our fight is with those who make the laws. Among them are racists, and they are fighting to reestablish political power so they can suppress the country's diversity. Like many others, you relaxed when we got a black man into the Oval Office. But the racists were working hard to regain control of Congress, which they did because you and many others don't realize how important it is to control both chambers of Congress."

"You blaming me?" Derrick said.

"I'm blaming you and all who didn't vote in the midterms. Every day we have to use the weapons that we are born with: our eyes to comprehend the things we see, our ears to understand the things we hear, our mouths to speak the truth, our hands to help others, our feet to walk a mile and stand in line for hours to vote if necessary. This project is critical—and I will fund it by myself if necessary. I own 33 percent of Third Eye Films. How much is that worth?"

Derrick's face turned downward.

Gladys asked, "How much do you need?"

"I need money for travel and to hire staff. The candidates will raise the money for their campaigns—but I will need funding in case we have a candidate that is short of money."

Derrick lifted his head in an obligated expression. "How much?"

"Ten million to start. Think of it as an investment for the Unity Corporation."

Derrick stared, considering. Five silent seconds passed. "I will give you the money."

Yvonne's eyes watered. She sat. "Thank you." She extended her arms and slowly rubbed her thumbs across Derrick's wrists. Her sanpaku eyes were glistening.

She stood and faced the group. "I read a book of poems by Nikki Giovanni that led me to think about the many white women who lost their lives for socializing with blacks during the Jim Crow era. Shouldn't there be a memorial for those women?

"But there isn't one for the white women that were lynched for socializing with blacks. Those pictures are hidden from the eyes of the world. But those who led the war against President Lincoln have highways and schools named after them. We need to bring the lynchings of white women to light. Not only is it good for blacks to know, but young white women too, that they might know what it means when someone says, *Make this country great again.*"

She locked her eyes on Derrick. "Make a movie about Peb Falls. She was a white woman who was tarred and feathered for socializing with blacks, and then lynched in 1897 for continuing to socialize with blacks."

Derrick nodded twice. "I hadn't heard of Peb Falls—but she sounds like a good movie."

"Her story is a very good movie. The spirit of the people who did that to her and others are walking around today in hunter wear and suits. One of them is running for president—and he might win."

With the thought of that possibility, Derrick peered across the group.

"Ma, you think John Donaldson can win?" Charlene said. "I don't think America will elect a racist after having a black president."

Yvonne shifted to face her daughter. "I've been following politics closely for the past twelve years, and I've watched a lot of the opposition news channel."

"You mean, XOF?"

"Yes. That is where Mr. Donaldson, with his loud and brash criticism of the black president, gained his political following."

"But you said the racists are no longer the majority."

"They're not. But the presidential election isn't decided by the popular vote. The electoral college chooses the president. John Donaldson turns off many. But so does his opponent. It's like choosing the lesser of two evils. When confronted with that choice, enough people might not vote or vote for the third-party candidate. That is how John Donaldson can win."

Derrick slid his index finger from under his bottom lip to under his chin. "He just might win."

Gladys interjected, "We need to hold a press conference to announce that we have reached the goal for Phase One, the opening of investments for the remaining three phases, and Yvonne's get-out-the-vote initiative."

"How soon?" Derrick asked.

"ASAP. Yvonne, do you have a name for your project?"

"Yes, I do."

"What is it?"

"Country Before Party!"

"I like that slogan!" Gladys said.

The others agreed.

* * *

Later that day, after Derrick's week-long guests had left, two detectives arrived.

Derrick led them into the living area where he sat on the white leather sofa that faced one side of the double-sided baronial fireplace. The detectives sat facing each other on his left and right in the matching side chairs.

"Mr. Williams, do you know how Mr. Mendendorf learned the whereabouts of his wife and children?"

"I do not. Ryan told me that his former boss, Arthur Kornish, had hired a private investigator."

"It's my understanding that you and Mr. Mendendorf were good friends. You didn't try to help him find his family."

"I didn't."

"Why?"

"Because of what he told me about his wife—she didn't love him. But I didn't have to tell him that. He knew. But he loved his kids. He wouldn't have killed them, or his wife. Ryan was a meek and godly man—a sincere born-again Christian."

"Knowing how much Mr. Mendendorf loved his kids, why didn't you help him find his children?"

"I didn't feel it was in his best interest."

"When was the last time that you spoke to Mr. Mendendorf?"

"A few days ago."

"What did you talk about?"

"The job."

"What about the job?"

"Daily procedures."

"How did Mr. Mendendorf feel about the FBI investigating the company?"

"Like all of us. It's frivolous. Ryan didn't have any concerns about the investigation because there isn't any dirt."

"Anything else you can tell us?"

"Just want to reiterate that Ryan didn't kill his wife and kids?"

"You say that like you know who did. Do you know?"

"If I did, I would've told you."

Both detectives gazed as if trying to read Derrick's thoughts.

"Mr. Williams, I have the feeling that there is something you're not telling us."

"I have the feeling that there is something you're not telling me."

The detective at his right closed his pocket notepad and stood. The detective across from him stood and remained silent, as he had throughout the questioning.

"Thank you, Mr. Williams, for your time. If we have any additional questions, we will contact you."

Derrick nodded and walked in front as the detectives followed him to the elevator, discreetly scanning the surroundings.

The detectives boarded the elevator, turned around, and faced Derrick's impassive expression.

After the doors had merged, Derrick kept his eyes on the elevator as if he expected the doors to open because he could tell they knew he hadn't told them everything.

The patter of slippers across the hardwood floor diverted his attention. Juna was walking toward him with a troubled face. She squirmed and said, "We safe?"

He wrinkled his brow and narrowed his eyes. "Why did you ask that?"

"Because people likes to hurt you. What if they start fire? How we get out on top floor?"

"A lot of VIPs live in this building. I doubt if they will take the risk of harming them. But if there is a fire, we have fire-resistant walls and a sprinkler system. On the roof is the helicopter pad. I have pilots on call 24/7. If needed, the chopper will be here in less than five minutes."

She pointed at the open windows.

"As I told you already, you can see outside, but the outside cannot see inside. The windows are also bulletproof glass."

He embraced her—kissed her. His hands gently gripped her arms. "If you want, you can go back to Hawaii. I won't be mad. I want you to feel safe."

Her monolid eyes watered. "I not leave you."

He smiled. "I love you, Juna."

"I love you, more. Promise me, we die together."

"We're not going to die."

"Promise me."

"I promise."

She peered into his eyes as if he was all of her happiness.

He lifted her into his arms and whirled. She giggled and playfully kicked her feet.

"Jacob, play Bryan Ferry," he said.

Juna was humming, "Don't stop..." as Derrick carried her into the bedroom.

CHAPTER 2

Inside the windowless four-cornered room, Arthur sat unconcerned in the brown, armless wooden chair at the matching six-foot table. Video monitors were visible from every angle.

Agent Simms, the long-faced, slightly bucktoothed man with bushy brows and moppy hair, faced Arthur.

On the left side of the table sat agent Daniels, a bald, round-faced, bulky man. On the other side sat agent Randall, a slender, dark-haired androgynous woman.

"Mr. Kornish," Agent Simms said, "let me remind you that it's a felony to lie to the FBI."

"I know. I will be as honest as I can."

"As honest as you can? What does that mean?"

Arthur chuckled slightly. "I will tell you all that I know."

"Good."

"Do I need to take an oath?"

"Not necessary. You are already under oath."

Arthur leaned back and stretched clasped hands on the table. "Okay, so what do you wanna know?"

"You told the police that the first time you talked to Ryan Mendendorf after his release from prison was about a month ago. Is that right?"

"Yes."

"Tell me about that encounter."

"I was in Soho, buying fruit from a street vendor when Ryan approached me. I was shocked to see him. He asked if I knew the whereabouts of his wife and kids. I told him that I didn't. I told the police the vendor was a witness to our conversation."

"Why was Ryan in Soho?"

"I don't know."

"Why were you in Soho?"

"I was there to buy fruit."

"Why did you go from Wall Street to Soho to buy fruit?"

"Because I like that vendor's fruit."

"Are you one of his regular customers?"

"It happened to be my first visit. I went to Soho because I tasted his peaches from a friend."

"Who's the friend?"

"I rather not say. It's a woman, and I'm a married man."

"When was the next time that you saw Ryan?"

"I invited him to an outing on my boat the following Saturday. He came but stayed for less than an hour. That was the last time I saw him."

"Did he ask you to help him find his wife, or did you tell him that you would help him find his wife?"

"I told him that I would ask around, but I didn't learn anything."

"You didn't learn the whereabouts of his wife and children?"

"No, I didn't. I tried."

"How did you try?"

"I asked around, but didn't learn anything?"

"Who did you ask?"

"Friends and former co-workers."

"Did you hire a private investigator to find Ryan's family?"

"Yes, but he didn't learn anything. I guess his wife and kids went deep into hiding when they learned that Ryan had been released from prison."

"Who was the private investigator?"

"A friend."

"What's the friend's name?"

"Anderson Schofield."

Agent Simms paused before he said, "Did you ask Ryan for confidential information on the finances of Third Eye Films?"

"I told him what was common knowledge—the company is under federal investigation and that if he had information on criminal activity that he should go to the FBI—but he said he was loyal to Mr. Williams and wouldn't betray him. I guess that's the reason why he killed his wife and kids, to be with them in death instead of going back to prison."

"How do you think Mr. Mendendorf was able to locate his wife and kids?"

"He probably hired a private detective, or Mr. Williams hired one for him."

"I'm sure your friend is very skilled. Do you believe Ryan or Mr. Williams could've hired a private detective better than your friend?"

"Maybe, because I only allocated a small amount for the investigation."

"Is there anything else you would like to tell us?"

"Not that I can think of."

"Anything you like to change from what you told us?"

"No. I've been truthful."

Agent Daniels reached into the side pocket of his blue suit jacket and placed a cell phone on the table.

Arthur's eyes widened. His bushy brows rose. *Whose phone is that?*

Agent Daniels had his eyes locked on Arthur. "Is there anything you would like to add or change on your answers to our questions?"

Arthur hesitated. *He's bluffing. They got nothing.* "I've told you all that I know."

Agent Daniels played the message. "Hi, Derrick. I called earlier but didn't leave a message. Arthur sent me the address of my wife and children. I'm outside their home now. But I'm afraid to knock on the door. Just calling to get your advice. Talk to you later."

Arthur's pupils grew. *Fuck! I was told that Ryan didn't leave any messages.*

"Mr. Kornish, you have committed a felony," Agent Daniels said. "Would you like to come clean and tell us what's going on here? Ryan said that you sent him the address—and he doesn't sound like a man with intentions to commit murder-suicide. Who killed Ryan and his family?"

"I-I d-don't know."

"Why did Ryan leave a message saying that you gave him the address?"

"I-I don't know."

"What do you know?"

"I-I don't know anything."

"Know this. You are under arrest for lying to the FBI."

"Under arrest?"

"You can get up to five years unless you decide to help us."

"Help you how?"

"Who else is involved?"

"Involved in what? I want to speak to my lawyer. I don't have anything more to say."

"Arthur, Arthur, Arthur," agent Randall said. "We know you have very powerful friends. Do you believe you will be safe when they learn of your arrest?"

"I want to speak to my attorney."

Within the hour, Arthur was out on bail. He attempted to contact Erich Hornsby and the other members of the council, but the encrypted lines were dead, and their home numbers were blocked.

Arthur's worry became fear.

*　*　*

The following morning, Hornsby assembled the council via encrypted Skype. "Arthur is the dead man walking. His dumb ass got the feds and reporters investigating a conspiracy. We need to lay low."

"Do you think he will flip?" Mr. Silverton asked.

Hornsby glared. "What's better—six months in the fenceless prison or six-feet under? Make sure Arthur receives that message from someone who doesn't know us."

Silverton nodded.

"Enough old news. I'm not happy about the national polls. What can we do?"

"Continue doing what we are doing," Murt Pointer said. "Our strategy isn't to win the popular vote but the electoral college, and we are in the position to win it."

"That's what you told me four years ago, and the black Muslim was reelected. He would win again if he could run again. What does that say about our country?"

Hornsby leaned forward with his small pale hands clasped on the wood table. His orange stone-face had its customary frown. "We need to take our country back to the days when niggers feared us."

"Amen," came from the mouths of a few before Samuel Hindenburg said, "It's time to make our country great again."

Hornsby led the chorus of claps before he said, "We have to do everything within our power to win this election. That includes accepting help from our foreign and domestic enemies."

"Donaldson has energized the George Wallace democrats who haven't voted in forty years," Murt said. "They will help us win Pennsylvania, Wisconsin, and Michigan."

"Win we must, or civil war will be our only option," Hornsby said. "And we cannot win the civil war without control of the Pentagon."

Jake Getz, Arthur's replacement, asked, "When we win the election, how long do we have to wait before the New Order?"

Hornsby shifted his reddish eyes. "To update you, Mr. Getz, when we regain control of the White House, we will assassinate Minister Kabir. His murder will lead to nationwide riots like when the fathers killed Dr. King. That will be our excuse to implement martial law.

"During that time, there will be an explosion at Camp David that will kill the president, vice-president, and the Speaker of the House. As secretary of state, I will be sworn in as president. In my address to the nation, I will accuse radical Islam as the perpetrators and arrest and detain all Muslims in this country.

"With the secretary of defense an ally, we will disband Congress, outlaw freedom of the press, burn the Constitution, remove all nonwhite immigrants, and slaughter every Jew and nigger. America will take its rightful place in the world as the Fourth Reich, with Russia replacing Italy, and China the new Japan."

The members stood and applauded.

After eight seconds of gloating, Hornsby gestured for them to sit.

They faced him and extended their right arm in the air with a straightened hand. "Hail Hornsby!" came from their mouths before they sat.

He nodded his approval. "The independent media is our biggest threat. They are the enemy of the people. Our plan will take three years to implement. We have to keep the eyes of the media on the left hand while we are using the right—so we have to keep our hands off of Derrick Williams until after the election."

Bart Henson, the owner of the largest energy company in America, said, "Williams is getting married next week."

Hornsby grinned. "Activate Boston. Let's see what comes of that. It'll be harder for the pastors to continue supporting an adulterer. Let him think that he has won the war. I want him relaxed for the kill."

Hornsby pointed his cratered chin upward. "Political power is our strength. If we lose it, we will lose our country. We must win this election! If we don't, the new Americans will come from shithole countries."

CHAPTER 3

"Ma, I told you that I want a small wedding. You got four hundred people on this list. I don't even know some of these people."

"Derrick, you have to invite the family. You will offend your investors if you don't invite every one of them to your wedding. On such short notice, most of them will not be able to attend, but they will appreciate the invite. It's also important to invite politicians and community leaders. Most of them will not be able to attend, but they will have an invite that they can bolster. It's also important to invite every employee at Third Eye Films and the staff at the Unity Corporation headquarters. They are members of your team, and you need them to feel special. Focus on your honeymoon. I got this. Do you trust me?"

"Of course, I trust you."

"Good. So don't question my decisions. You're the one that said, 'I'm smarter and greater than you.' If you believe that, you won't question my decisions."

She gripped his upper arms and leaned slightly backward. "We are in this fight together. To win, you have to allow others to be your hand. You have to trust the decisions made by the members of your team. If you can't trust us to handle small matters, how can you trust us to handle the major? You cannot micromanage and expect to be an effective leader."

"I'm adjusting."

"You're not adjusting. You believe all your decisions are right. Don't deceive yourself."

"Ma, I'm not deceiving myself. My decisions are right. God is guiding me."

"God is guiding you, but that doesn't make all your decisions right. God was guiding Abraham, but Abraham's decision not to cast out Ishmael was wrong. God had to correct him. God guided David, but David made poor decisions.

"You have wise counselors around you, so don't close your ears to our advice. The Bible says, 'Where no counsel is, the people fall; but in the multitude of counsellors there is safety.' (Proverbs 11:14). God has blessed you to have a multitude of wise counselors around you. Use us."

"Point made. But how will I know when I should take someone else's advice?"

"You need to keep an open mind. An open mind will weigh the pros and cons to make a wise decision. Your biggest threat is you."

"Me?" he said with his forehead and nose scrunched.

"Yeah, you! The devil is trying to use your wisdom against you."

Puzzled, he said, "How can the devil do that?"

"By making you believe that you don't need counsel."

Derrick was concentrating on those words when she said, "There is a thin line between a wise man and a fool."

"Minister Kabir said that."

"You're not the only one who listens to Minister Kabir."

He smiled, held her hands, and tilted his head to the right. "I'm blessed to have you as my mother."

She kissed him on the forehead and led him by the hand onto the terrace that overlooked Central Park.

She leaned with her arms on the black iron railing and pointed with her nose. "This is a beautiful world. But the Scripture says, 'Whosoever, therefore, will be a friend of the world is the enemy of God.'" (James 4:4)

Derrick turned his head to face her. "Ma. Why are you saying that to me?"

"Because I need you to stay focused. Your enemies have retreated but are not defeated. Enjoy the blessings that God has given you, but don't fall in love with the world or the things in it."

"Ma, you know I won't. Why are you telling me this?"

"Because you need to hear it. Some of the greatest men of God have fallen to a seductive woman. Adam, Samson, David, Solomon, and modern-day leaders whose names I don't want to mention."

"I'm getting married on Saturday. Juna is the only woman I want and need."

"I'm very happy to hear that. She loves you more than she loves herself. She's not my concern—you are."

"Me? Why?"

"Because you are one of the precious lives called to fight the powers that be on earth, and you are winning. That is angering the devil's children. They will use all their power to stop you. But only you can stop you from succeeding."

He scrunched his forehead. "Only I can stop me from succeeding? Elaborate?"

"By becoming complacent and following the nature of your manhood. The Scripture says, '...and the adulteress will hunt for the precious life.' (Proverbs 6:26). Hunt! Like a bloodhound with her nose to the ground, the adulteress hunts for the precious life. You are the prey. She will try to use your kindness as the weakness to seduce you.'"

"Are you speaking of someone in particular? I know you still think that I'm in love with Suzanne."

"Are you?"

"I'm not in love with her."

"I hope so. But the adulteress can be anyone you know or don't know."

"I won't become a victim—and I won't stop myself from succeeding."

"Good. I wouldn't be a wise mother if I didn't say these things. You are young, rich, handsome, smart, and full of faith and charity. There are lots of women looking for a man like you—and they don't care if you are married because they believe that they can make you fall in love with them. Women are more confident than most men."

"I'm a one-woman man!"

"I believe that. You are going against your nature, and I'm proud of that."

"My nature? You think man's nature is adultery?"

"I'm going to ask you a question, and please be honest. In the past two days, have you seen a woman that you were sexually attracted to besides Juna?"

His head tilted upward for two seconds, then returned. "Yes, but I didn't and won't pursue."

"Did you feel lust?"

"I-I thought about it for a second and moved on—that's natural."

"When you are married, do you think you will experience the same when you see a woman that sexually attracts you?"

"I will, but I won't touch."

"You don't have to touch to commit adultery. Jesus said, 'But I say unto you that whosoever looketh on a woman to lust after her hath committed adultery with her already in his heart.' (St. Matthew 5:28). Our thoughts and feelings are seen by the mirrors within us: that which reflects the truth in our hearts. God sees our true intentions when he looks at us in the mirror."

"So, when I am a married man and look at a woman that I find sexually attractive, according to that Scripture, I have committed adultery in my heart?"

"No. The Scripture says, 'whosoever looketh on a woman to lust after her hath committed adultery with her already in his heart.' To 'lust after her' is to pursue her. If you pursue then change your mind or she turns you away, you committed adultery in your heart because that was your initial intention. But if you look at her and feel a sexual attraction but don't pursue or accept her pursuit, then you haven't lusted after her. Like you always say, nothing can precede what the flesh feels. It's natural for a married man and woman to see someone that sexually attracts them. But the sin can only occur if you turn the feeling into action."

"If you don't control your urges, your urges will control you. I was eight when you first told me that. I remember you saying that all the time. I remember when you said some of our urges leads to hell. You said our eyes, hands, and mouth bring an urge into existence. I was listening to your life lessons." His eyes glistened. "I will not allow my eyes, or hands, or mouth, or penis to lead me astray. But there is one thing that I have learned: all things that appear to be sin in the eyes of man isn't sin in the eyes of God, because the end justifies the means if the end is righteous.'"

"Amen," his mother said.

"Now, can I ask you a personal question?"

"What is it?"

"Do you have a man in your life?"

"Not yet, and I'm not looking. I am happy alone. Of course, it would be nice to have a husband. If it's God's will, he will appear. Until then, I'm keeping my eyes on the prize."

"And what is the prize?"

"The new earth. A place where all races share the love for one another. A world where all countries are under God's government."

Derrick's eyes were smiling. "I'm giving you an extra twenty million dollars to fund your project."

Yvonne's eyes widened, and her lips curved upward. She hugged him. "Thank you! I'm happy that you believe in me."

"As you said, God has surrounded me with wise counselors. Political power is a necessity for the Unity Corporation's success."

"Yes, it is—and we are going to get it."

* * *

The white satin aisle runner divided the four hundred white folding chairs on the blue-pearl marble tile. Under the seven-foot wedding arch covered in white roses, Amari stood in a black robe with a black four-pointed tassel hat. The sunset was the backdrop.

Yvonne was sitting on the first seat of the front row and shifted her eyes to Derrick, who faced her in a tailored black two-piece shawl-collar tuxedo and satin bow tie. Blue was standing next to him in matching attire.

The renowned pianist played the wedding march, and Yvonne turned her head and gazed at Charlene, who slowly stepped as the maid of honor in a yellow V-neck beaded mesh gown. Behind her, two little girls in white lace dresses dropped handfuls of red rose petals from their oversized white wicker baskets.

When the pianist cued the bride, the eyes in every seat turned to see. In the white ball gown with off-shoulder lace sleeves and a heart-shaped lace back and royal-length train, Juna gracefully came forward. She was holding her bouquet in the shape of a diamond.

Yvonne's eyes watered and lifted toward the orange-and-blue sky. *She's beautiful, Cedric. I know you're watching. I know you're proud of your son.*

Beverly was sitting on the row behind Yvonne. She leaned into Diane's ear and whispered, "He's only known the girl for three weeks. It won't last."

Diane whispered, "Ma, shut up!"

The pronouncement ended with a standing ovation that continued until the bride and groom stepped off the terrace. Derrick immediately lifted Juna and carried her in his arms into their bedroom. The faces of her family and friends in the Philippines were on the screen that faced them. Nenita, with her baby in her arms and husband closely behind, entered the room.

After a few minutes of congenial conversation, Derrick left in search of Blue and Michael. Congratulatory hugs and daps from guests delayed his search.

He was chatting with Cynthia and her husband when Judy and Michael approached. He excused himself and hugged Judy and dapped with Michael.

"You look good as a couple. I love it," Derrick said.

Both were smiling and replied, "Thank you."

After chatting a minute with both, Derrick pulled Michael to the side. "I heard you are going to West Virginia."

"Yeah. I'm meeting Judy's parents while we are at Massanutten Mountain on Labor Day weekend."

"Be careful. There are lots of gun-toting far-right-wingers up in those mountains, and they know you're one of my brothers."

"I'll be careful."

They dapped and Michael led Judy on the tour of the penthouse.

Derrick and Blue were chatting while the guests were socializing on both floors.

"Heyyy," Shareese shouted and scooted into Derrick's embrace.

"Blue, this is Shareese. She works at the Unity Corporation."

"Nice to meet you. I know why they call you Blue."

"The darker the berry, the sweeter the juice," he said.

"You got that right," she replied and laughed.

Blue smiled. "I like you already."

"Thank you. I like you too." She swung her close-set eyes to Derrick. "This place is way too big for just you and your wife. One floor is too much, but two... How many children are you planning to have?"

He smiled. "As many as the Lord gives me. I bought this place as an investment, but my wife likes it, so I'll keep it."

"Well, it's off-the-hook. Okay, let me go and socialize with some of these fine men up in here. I'll see you later."

Seconds later, Charlene and Amari approached.

Derrick immediately extended his hand. "Thanks again for marrying me on your Sabbath day."

"You're Jewish?" Blue said.

"Yes. I'm Hebrew-Christian."

"I thought it was a sin for Jews to work on the Sabbath."

"We follow the teachings of Jesus. It's lawful to do good and save life on the Sabbath—St. Luke 6:9. Overseeing a marriage is doing good because what God has joined together, let no man keep apart."

"Cool."

Charlene hugged her brother and kissed him on the cheek. "Congratulations. You have a beautiful wife."

He broadened his smile. "Thanks. You look beautiful too."

She smiled and excitedly led Amari by the hand down the spiral staircase.

"Your sister is in love," Blue said.

"She found the right one for her."

"I was hoping I was the right one."

"Everything we hope for isn't meant for us. Yours will come. Aren't you still sharing your bone?"

"Yeah, but I'm ready to fall in love."

Derrick's closed lips curved upward.

"Since you are leaving tomorrow on your thirty-day honeymoon, let me update you," Blue said. "The two films we owe to end the contract are done."

Surprised, Derrick said, "Already?"

"Yeah. I was working on it when I told you that I wasn't."

"Why did you keep me in the dark?"

"Because you need to stop micromanaging. You need to trust me."

"I trust you."

"Not fully. You think I'm prioritizing my record label. But Third Eye Films is priority number one."

"I'm happy to know that. My mother told me that I need to stop micromanaging. She said I need to trust my partners."

"You do. Now that you have allowed your mother to invest in the Corporation, can I?"

Derrick peered into Blue's eyes. "Yes, you can invest."

"Good. I want to invest in Phase Two, Three, and Four."

"Okay. Holler at Gladys."

"Cool. I'm working on our next independent film."

"What is it?"

"Hannibal."

"The African king who conquered Europe?"

"Word."

"I like that. I have another movie in mind."

"Another like *Peb Falls*?"

"Nah. The Maccabees."

"The Maccabees? Who are they?"

"Google them. We'll talk about it later."

Derrick glanced at his left wrist. "It's time for the wedding party pictures. Find my mother and Charlene, and meet us on the Central Park terrace."

"Cool."

***

Eight-person round tables had white linen, clear votive candles, and 24-kt. gold-plated bamboo-handled flatware. Each chair had an ivory tulle wrapped with satin ribbon. Two rows of white sky lanterns replaced the runner and divided the tables. White linen and fresh bouquets in six-inch crystal vases covered the wedding table.

The open bar had top-shelf at five stations: one on the wedding/reception terrace, two in the top floor open space, and two on the floor below. Servers wore tuxedos and carried trays of hors d'oeuvres on both floors.

Shareese, seated at one of the reception tables, plucked the satay beef skewer and three grilled shrimp skewers. She also had two empty shots of tequila in front of her.

A well-dressed middle-aged man sat directly across. He had salmon canapes and stuffed hors d'oeuvres on his small gold-rimmed plate.

Shareese pointed. "That stuffed hors d'oeuvre looks good. What is it called?"

"Cream cheese stuffed mushrooms."

"I need to try some of that."

"Take one of mine."

"Nah, you will probably think I'm greedy."

"No, I won't."

"Yes, you will. You won't admit it, but in your mind, you'll be saying that girl is greedy, that's why she's fat."

"I'm not like that. I like my women healthy like you."

"Mmm. You hitting on me?"

"What you think?"

"I think you're a one-minute man."

"A one-minute man?"

"Yeah, you look like a one-minute man."

"What does a one-minute man look like?"

"You. When was the last time you had some?"

"Uh, th-the l-last time?"

"I know for sure now that you're a one-minute man. I didn't come all the way from Hawaii to meet a one-minute man. I had enough of them in high school."

"I'm not a one-minute man. You want me to prove it."

"Hmm. What's your shoe size?"

"Eleven and a half."

She pursed her lips, narrowed her eyes, and tilted her head to the side. "I-I'll think about it."

Shareese shifted her eyes toward the tables on the other side of the sky lanterns. *Damn, who's that James Dean look-alike? Hmm, he likes the full figure too.* She scanned his fingers. *Not married. Um, added.* She nodded with her lips puckered.

After the traditional bride and groom dance that included the opportunity for guests to dance solo with them, Shareese, in her long neon-lime loose dress, got the party started when she broke out the *Double Dab*—then *One Leg Up*.

"Heyyy!" she shouted as Ruben joined her. "Break it down for me, baby."

Ruben challenged her with the *Stab,* and she matched him.

"Back that ass up," he said.

Shareese bent over, grabbed her ankles, and made her ass clap. "Pull up to that bumper, bay-b."

Ruben didn't hesitate.

* * *

On the first morning as a married man, Derrick stood barefoot on the bedroom terrace in gray, fitted boxers. He was gazing at the blue and yellow dawn. Memories from days past had pushed tears to the edge.

He shifted his watering eyes toward the bed and smiled. Juna lay naked on top of the white sheets, seemingly sound asleep.

He entered the opened terrace door and stood at the side of the platform bed. The dawn's light glowed on her chestnut skin.

Dear God, protect my wife before me. Keep her under the shadow of your wings. Continue to guide her in all your wisdom, and add comfort when needed. In Jesus' name, I pray.

Her body stretched as if she could hear his thoughts. But she didn't wake.

He smiled and softly whispered, "I love you."

His eyes shifted to the astral view at the head of the bed. *Thank you, God.*

He looked at the purple sky that covered the early morning clouds, and his biological father and brothers came to mind as if he could see them in the light of dawn.

Daddy, I wish I had seen you one time in the flesh. But when I look in the mirror, I see you as my flesh. I know you live in me on earth as I live in you in heaven. My dream is your dream. My life is the one that you sacrificed your life for me to have. I love you because I love myself.

Junior, I regret that we weren't close in our youth. But I love you. Now that you are not here, I realize how much I love you. There are many things I want to say to you, and I will because your seed will live in the flesh again when your sister gives birth.

Mister, when you went to heaven without me, I was mad at you. I missed you so much. But you never left me. I kept hearing your voice, and that comforted me. You made me study. You made me pray. You made me rich. You saved me from that devil woman. You are my guardian angel, and my firstborn is the vessel for your spirit to live again in the flesh.

He lowered his eyes to Juna's bubble rear and felt the urge but went back into the July air. Restless, he lay on the terrace lounger and watched the purple sky mingle with the orange. He lifted his earplugs from the small white cabinet that was next to the lounger, inserted them, and said, "Play DIDI HAN." He smiled and thought about the things that might be on Juna's mind.

When the song ended, he said, "Phone Blue."
"What's up," Blue said, seemingly awake.
"I'm married, brah."
"Yes, you are. Any regrets?"
"Nah. I'm happy. Very happy. I love her."
"She's perfect for you, brah."
"Who's that rapping with the sax?"
"Westside Gunn."
"I like that cut."
"I'll text it to you."
"Bet. Why are you up so early? I thought I was waking you up."
"Been up all night."
"What time did you leave?"
"Around one."
"And you're still up? You must have a girl with you."
"Yeah, I do."
"Anybody, I know?"

Blue paused before he said, "Shareese."

"Shareese! Shareese is with you?"

"Yeah, brah."

Derrick chuckled. "Ah, right, brah. I'll let you get back. We can chat later."

"Cool."

Derrick ended the call with a smile. *Shareese and Blue. Oh my God.*

CHAPTER 4

The Ocean Villas in Newport, Rhode Island, welcomed Derrick and Juna at the start of their thirty-day honeymoon. Two local bodyguards on eight-hour shifts followed when they left the doors of the villa.

The couple were strolling arm-in-arm along the railed world-famous Cliff Walk. The morning breeze carried the fresh air across their faces. The sound of cawing seagulls and the ocean exploding on the rocks enhanced the scenic views.

Juna's head lay on Derrick's upper arm. "Do you love me?" she asked, as if she needed reassurance.

Derrick frowned and halted their leisurely pace. "Why did you ask that?"

She lowered her eyes.

He lifted her chin with his fingers. "Tell me? Why did you ask that?"

"Because I heard Grandma Beverly say, you should've married a black girl."

"I married the woman that I love. You didn't marry my family. You married me. We are one now. The only person that comes before you is God. You even come before my mother. I'm serious."

"But you always talk about the importance of black people sticking together."

"You're black. The people in the Philippines are descendants of the Negritos."

"I know, but Filipinos don't like to be reminded of that."

"Why? Don't run from the truth. That is how the Filipinos looked before the Spanish and Japanese occupations."

"I know. Maybe that why I like black man."

"Don't ever question my love for you. When I see you, I see a gift from God. He gave me everything that I need and desire in a woman. He gave me my soulmate; he gave me the happiness I didn't have."

"I sorry," she said with a tear rolling slowly from each eye.

He embraced her and gingerly stroked the silky black hair that hung over her shoulders. "I will always love you, Juna. You are my best friend."

"I always love you more."

They kissed, returned to their hotel room, and ate lunch, dinner, and breakfast in bed.

* * *

While her son was on his honeymoon, Yvonne was vetting candidates, attending nationwide political events, and recruiting political science majors from the historically black colleges and universities (HBCUs). After attending a political rally in Florida, she met with the democratic candidate for president.

"Thank you for accepting my invitation, Mrs. Dunbar. I'm a fan of your son's movies and support his efforts to empower black communities."

"Thank you, Mrs. Benton," Yvonne said without enthusiasm.

Mrs. Benton's expression soured. Her aged hooded eyes narrowed. "I'm sure you are aware that my opponent is a racist and unqualified to be president. I am hopeful that I will receive an endorsement from the Unity Corporation."

"I'm sorry. We cannot commit our endorsement at this time."

"Why? I have a long history of support for the black community."

"We haven't forgotten that you tried to steal the nomination eight years ago."

"Ah, that wasn't personal. I was only using my options as any candidate would've in a close election."

"We didn't see it that way. We certainly are not endorsing your opponent, but we cannot endorse you either. I can honestly say that I will vote for you, and I look forward to meeting with you after you win the election. I want to discuss criminal justice reform, childcare, and other issues that affect the black community."

With a frown that reflected in her eyes, Mrs. Benton said, "I thank you for your vote."

Yvonne didn't want the meeting to end on the sour note, so she said, "Mrs. Benton, we cannot endorse, but we will be working to help you win. I want to send some of my staff to work with the members of your campaign if that is okay?"

Mrs. Benton gruffed, "If you cannot openly endorse me, then you cannot help me."

"Sooo, you are rejecting my offer?"

"You haven't presented an offer."

"Thank you, Mrs. Benton. Hopefully, you will become the first woman president." Yvonne smiled, shook her hand and the hand of her campaign manager, and walked out of the hotel suite, feeling the stares filled with contempt coming from Mrs. Benton and her campaign manager.

Yvonne boarded the elevator, and when the doors closed, she said to herself, "She won't get my vote."

* * *

A week later, by invitation, Yvonne flew to Georgia and met with Randy Jefferson, the candidate for the US Senate.

"Mrs. Dunbar, I heard the Unity Corporation is considering endorsing the third-party candidate. I hope that is not true. I'm the only black candidate in this race."

"Mr. Jefferson, the Unity Corporation is throwing our support behind the independent candidate."

"Whaaat! A white woman! Our communities have been led to believe the Unity Corporation supports black people and black businesses. Has the Unity Corporation changed? If so, I need to know about it so I can share the news during my travel into the black communities across this state."

"No need. We are holding a press conference with Bethany Turner on Thursday morning."

He frowned without trying to hide it. "I hope you reconsider because the Unity Corporation will look like a sell-out if you endorse a white person over a black person who has a long history of support in the black communities."

Yvonne clasped her hands and placed her elbows on the oak table. Her brothers, Steve and Ruben, stood behind her.

"Mr. Jefferson, the political arm for the Unity Corporation isn't committed to a person's race. The candidates we endorse are first and foremost without corruption. We support those who are not afraid to speak out against a popular politician if he or she violates the law or ethics of the office. Our candidates choose country over party."

"But that's not how it works in the real world. I think you are criticizing me for not condemning the congressman for the allegations made against him. I can't condemn someone because of allegations. I would be a fool to anger his voters when I need their votes."

"Those were facts and not allegations. Mrs. Turner needed his voters, but she chose right over wrong. That caused her to lose the Democratic primary against you. She is the candidate we are endorsing."

His expression turned angry.

"Mr. Jefferson, we don't endorse politicians that look the other way because he or she is afraid of being voted out of office, or not into office. The press conference on Thursday will lay out in detail our reasons for endorsing Mrs. Turner."

She left the office unconcerned that he had become an enemy.

* * *

Inside her North Carolina home, Yvonne sat on the stone-colored, oversized chair. A flute that had a third of white wine remaining in it sat on the round, glass end table catercorner to the matching sofa. Tunes by Nina Simone serenaded the contemporary furnished room.

As if she was facing God, Yvonne said, "Lord, hear my prayer. Protect my son and his wife. Watch over my daughter. Keep me on the right path. Help me to be successful in all my projects. Without you, I can accomplish nothing. Without you, nothing good can happen in this world. I am with you unto the end."

Minutes later, her phone rang, and she voice-activated the portal.

"Hey, Charlene!"

"Hi, Ma. You okay?"

"I'm okay."

"What's that book you're reading? I like the cover, but it looks different from what you usually read."

"It's *the Breedline Series* by Shana Congrove. The story is science fiction and fantasy. You're right, it's not my usual read, but I met the author at a book festival and decided to buy her book. This is my third book by her. You should read, *the Breedline Series*. It's very good."

"If you like it, then I know I will, so I'll buy it."

Yvonne smiled.

"Ma, why don't you start dating? Mr. Hollister likes you a lot, but you keep ignoring him. He's a handsome man."

"I'm not interested in dating right now, baby. I have other things on my mind."

"Ma, you're only fifty-one years old. I know you're lonely."

"I'm married to the church. The church makes me happy."

"Church makes me happy too, but I still need the company of a man. You need a man in your life. I like Mr. Hollister. He's your type. I don't understand why you won't at least go on a date with him."

"Why do you and your brother keep pressing me to date?"

"Because we don't want you to be alone?"

"I'm not alone. Jesus is with me. If meant to be, God will send me a man, and I will recognize him. Right now, it's time for me to be me."

"What do you mean?"

"Let me explain it this way. When I look at my life in the mirror, I see moments of happiness and sadness, and things that make me question the fairness of life. But when I think about my life with the spiritual mind, everything that occurred has brought me to this moment. A political activist is my calling."

"Ma, I see a whole new side of you."

"And what's that?"

"Angela Davis-like."

"She is a part of me—and Harriet Tubman, and Rosa Parks, and Deborah in the book of Judges. We all walk in the same spirit."

Charlene's mouth didn't open, but thoughts of concern reflected from her eyes.

Yvonne noticed and said, "You have heard this side of me. Now you are seeing this side of me. Our lives are in the mirror, but there are some things we see that others can't and some things that are latent until the hour the Lord calls us. The hour of my calling has come."

"Ma, I don't like the way you are talking. Why can't you just be a mom? Let God handle the world."

"I am letting God handle the world. He uses us to speak His truth to others. He uses us to show His love to others. He uses us to represent Him in human flesh."

"I know. I just want somebody else's mother to be chosen. It's dangerous, Ma! They're gonna try and kill you too."

"Baby, you cannot live if you're afraid to die."

"I don't want you to die. Our family has seen enough death. Mister died. Junior died. My father died. Derrick's father died. They want to kill Derrick, and now they will want to kill you. Why can't you just stay in the shadows? Why do you have to be on the front line?"

"Because that's where God wants me."

"Is it God, or you? I think you're bored. That's why I want you to have a man in your life."

Without breaking eye contact, Yvonne closed the book and set it next to her. "Charlene, I've been hearing God speak directly to me since I was fourteen. I'm not going to stop listening now. I know you are concerned. But I'm doing what makes me happy. I'm fulfilling my purpose in life."

Charlene had tears at the edge. Two seconds later, a tear rolled from each eye. "I'm just scared for you, Mom. If you and Derrick die, I'll be all alone."

"You are never alone with God. Baby, I'm not going to die before my time."

"Junior didn't think it was his time to die, but he died—he died before his time."

"Remember when I told you and Junior to think before you speak because sometimes you can't take back the words that come from out of your mouth?"

"I remember that. We were eight years old the first time you told us."

"Junior died because he didn't take that life lesson to heart. All of his apologies didn't matter to the person that he offended. The world is a dangerous place because people are unable to control their urges. If he were able to control his, he would be alive today."

"Ma, you blaming Junior for his death? He was hot-headed, but that doesn't excuse the person that murdered him."

"No, it doesn't. But if you allow the devil to use your temper against you, he will lead you into harm's way. I told that to Junior many times."

Charlene cried. "Ma, you are blaming Junior for his death."

"Baby, I know you don't want to hear it, but Junior contributed to his death."

Charlene's tears increased. "M-Ma, h-how, c-can you say that?"

"It's the truth, Charlene. The serpent didn't force Eve to eat the forbidden fruit. Eve didn't force Adam to eat the forbidden fruit. Their father-God told them what would happen if they did, and they disobeyed Him. God didn't cause the evil in this world. We did. God often gets the blame when we are the ones to blame."

Charlene was wiping her tears. "Who is the blame for Mister's death?"

"Remember what you told me after Junior's death? Those words brought me back from a dark place because you reminded me that there is a positive side to every negative thing."

"That doesn't answer who is the blame for Mister's death."

Yvonne paused. She didn't want to answer.

"Ma, say it."

"The final blame is always on the person whose hand causes the death. But Derrick contributed because he didn't obey me. He opened the door for Shirley to enter the house. That led to the altercation with her brother that resulted in Mister's death."

"Ma, Derrick was only five years old. You can't blame him."

"I'm not blaming him. Mister is dead because JT shot him, not Derrick. I-I also contributed to Mister's death because I left my five-year-old son at home alone."

Charlene sniffled. "No, Ma, you can't blame yourself for that. You had to work. There was nothing else you could've done."

"I could've quit my job."

"What would that have done? From what you told me about Mister, he would've quit school and started working to help pay the bills. That little bit of money wouldn't've been enough, so he might've started selling drugs."

Yvonne was quiet in her solemn expression. Memories that she didn't want to recall had surfaced. Her face drooped, with more tears. Her thoughts turned to moments with Cedric, Charles, Mister, and Junior.

Charlene sobbed with her. The tears of mother and daughter at odds unified them at that moment.

Charlene sniffled. "You're right, Ma. Sometimes we contribute to the bad things that happen to us. I let James touch my private parts, and he almost raped me."

"But that's not an excuse for what James did. Junior embarrassed Roberto, but that wasn't a justifiable reason to kill him, neither JT killing Mister. Both were cold-blooded murder. The reason I didn't file charges against James wasn't that you were pleading for me not to."

"Was it because it was partially my fault?"

"No. I didn't file charges because you told me that when you said, stop, he did."

"I wasn't totally honest, Ma. When I told him to stop, he didn't. But when I started crying, he did."

"Why didn't you tell me the whole story? How many times have I told you that if you don't tell the whole truth, you haven't told the truth?"

"If I had told you the truth, you would've filed charges."

"That's right—because he intended to rape you. How did you tell him to stop?"

"What you mean?"

"How did you say it? Did you whisper or yell?"

"I repeatedly yelled, 'No! Stop!'"

Yvonne's eyes watered as if she could see that moment on her daughter's face. "Baby, you should've told me the truth."

Charlene's eyes turned downward. "According to your analysis, Ma, I'm guilty too."

"Keep your head up. Let me make this clear: You are guilty of putting yourself in that situation. But you are not the blame for his actions. He betrayed your trust in him. He intended to rape you because he ignored your repeated screams to stop. He was only thinking about himself at that moment. He didn't care about how you were feeling."

She murmured, "He stopped when I cried."

"I thank God and not him for that."

"Can we talk about something more pleasant?"

Yvonne smiled. "How is your relationship with Amari?"

* * *

On Derrick and Juna's honeymoon they spent three nights each in Newport, Chicago, New Orleans, San Antonio, Aspen, San Francisco, Los Angeles, Charleston, Miami, and San Juan, and one night in Orlando.

Charlene and Amari were at Derrick's penthouse when he and Juna returned. After the four had viewed pictures and videos, Charlene and Juna went shopping. Derrick and Amari sat in the open space on the first of the two floors.

Derrick was sitting on the sofa with his legs stretched and ankles crossed. "I like to know more about prophet William and the Church of God."

Amari leaned forward with arms on thighs and fingers locked. "Prophet William was a deacon in a Baptist church when he received his revelation to preach the tribes of Israel are the former slaves in America. In 1896, he reestablished the *Church of God and Saints of Christ* under the Hebrew-Christian denomination."

"Reestablished?"

"Yes. The Church of God and Saints of Christ were the Christians slain by Nero. We are living the ancient of days in modern times. The prophet named Washington, DC, Jerusalem; Philadelphia, Zion; New York City, Babylon; and all of the USA, Israel. He brought back the Ancient of Days."

"The Ancient of Days? Elaborate."

"Daniel chapter seven, verses 9, 13, and 22. The Ancient of Days is Christ, the Word, the Old and New Testaments, and the repeat of days that includes the Diaspora and split of Israel."

Derrick nodded in consideration. "So, the American slave trade was the new Diaspora?"

"Yes."

"That's why there are different sects of black Hebrews in America."

"Yes. There is even a split in the church reestablished by prophet William."

"So, we are God's chosen."

"We are the very elect. There is the elect and the very elect. John saw a number which no man could number of all peoples, languages, and nations. Those are the elect. But the hundred and forty-four thousand that stand with the Lamb on Mount Zion are the very elect—the twelve tribes of Israel."

Derrick leaned forward with elbows on knees and hands clasped between his legs. His tongue twisted to the side in his closed mouth. He stared. "Makes sense," he said.

"But do you believe it to be true?"

"I do. I believe I am from the lost tribe of Judah."

Amari nodded. "Israel is not a land. Jacob was named Israel, so wherever the seed of Jacob travels, Israel travels. We believe when the Romans destroyed Jerusalem in 70 A.D., the tribe of Judah followed the coastline into the previously undiscovered land known today as South Africa. If you look at the early maps of South Africa, you will see towns named Jerusalem and Bethlehem, even Babylon. We weren't heathens on the slave ships. We knew God."

"What happened to the other tribes?"

"Some fled into Ethiopia and other parts of Africa to escape the genocide."

"So, who are the people in the land the earth calls Israel?"

"Greeks that worshipped with the Jews (St. John 12:20)."

"They converted?"

"Yes."

"Are they counted among the twelve tribes of Israel on Mt. Zion?"

"I don't speak outside the Scriptures. It's written, 'For he is not a Jew who is one outwardly; neither is that circumcision, which is outward in flesh; But he is a Jew, who is one inwardly; and circumcision is that of the heart, in the spirit and not in the letter; whose praise is not of men, but of God.' (Romans 2:28-29). That is to say if they believe in the Lord Jesus Christ, then they are counted among the twelve tribes of Israel—because the true Jew is inward, and the circumcision is in their heart and spirit.'"

Derrick leaned back, with questions in his mind.

"Please share your thoughts?" Amari said.

Derrick leaned forward, arms on thighs and fingers locked. "Your church is a bigger threat to the powers that be than any church on the earth."

"I know. But we are not seen as a threat because we are not preaching from the mountaintop."

"Why not? Why are you hiding the light of your candle?"

"I am not hiding our candle. It's not my calling to preach to the world. Prophet William was the world's evangelist. I'm keeping the church without spot or wrinkle until the Anointed has risen. He will preach on the mountaintop. Like you, I don't believe in coincidences."

"What are you hinting at, Amari?"

"You know. I saw the expression on your face when you came to our church. You thought we were a cult and were ready to leave, but quickly realized that we aren't. I felt your spirit embrace the service as if it was a part of your previous life. I could see in your eyes that you wanted to sit in one of those three seats. What stopped you?"

"Maybe it was an urge not meant to be."

"How could that be, when our church is everything you believe in?"

Derrick didn't fight the truth. "I didn't join because I believe the church is the body. I believe we are the temple of God."

"That is true. It's written, 'Nevertheless, the Most High dwelleth not in temples made with hands, as saith the prophet. Heaven is my throne, and earth is my footstool. What house will ye build me? saith the Lord. Or what is the place of my rest? Hath not my hand made all these things?' (Acts 7:48-50) It's also written in the book of Revelation after John describes the new Jerusalem that descends out of heaven, 'And I saw no temple in it; for the Lord God Almighty and the Lamb are the temple of it.'" (Revelation 21:22)

"It's good to know you are familiar with those Scriptures. I didn't think you were."

"I'm disappointed to learn that you underestimated my knowledge of the word. The church as an edifice is not a necessity—but fellowship is—and the building exists today for that purpose. It's written, 'Then they that gladly received his word were baptized; and the same day there were added unto them about three thousand souls. And they continued steadfastly in the apostles' doctrine and fellowship, and in breaking of bread, and in prayers.' (Acts 2:41-42) The churches and temples made with man's hands are for the fellowship of ministering to the saints and continuing tradition."

"You think that God has called me to join your church?"

"It's not what I think. It's what you believe."

Derrick considered.

*　*　*

Charlene and Juna were meandering among the crowd in Columbus Circle. The two armed bodyguards were following closely as they frequently entered shops.

With shopping bags in both hands on the down escalator, Juna leaned and whispered, "I'm pregnant."

Charlene's mouth gaped with her eyes widened. "Wow! You sure?"

Juna smiled. "Ooo, yes."

Charlene waited until they stepped off the elevator before she gave her the joyous embrace. Their bodies were rapidly swinging side to side.

"I'm so happy for you. Does Derrick know?"

"Not yet. I tell him tonight. I'm sure now."

"You took a pregnancy test when you were inside the pharmacy?"

"Ooo, yes."

"Wow! Awesome! Congratulations, Sis! I can't wait to see Derrick's face when he finds out."

Like maternal sisters, they wrapped arms, exited the mall, and skipped around the Columbus Circle trees.

At the darker stage of twilight, Charlene and Juna returned to Central Park West. The effervescent doorman greeted them and opened the door. The bodyguards didn't follow when they entered the private elevator.

"I want you to tell him as soon as you see him," Charlene said with a happy face.

"I'm shy."

"Just say it. He'll do the rest."

When the doors of the elevator opened on the second floor of the penthouse, Derrick and Amari were facing them across the sixty-foot inlaid marble foyer.

With two shopping bags in each hand, Charlene excitedly ran into Amari's embrace.

Juna shyly stepped toward Derrick and put down her three shopping bags.

"What's wrong?" he asked.

"Nothing. I'm happy. I love you."

He patted her lips. "I love you too. Now tell me, what's wrong?"

Charlene had her smiling eyes on Juna, Amari looked curious, Derrick had a blank expression.

"Go ahead, tell him," Charlene said gleefully.

With mixed thoughts, looking at Juna, Derrick asked, "Tell me what?"

"I'm pregnant."

"YES!" He lifted her to his lips and spun her around. He lowered her to the floor. "I love you." He kissed her, then kissed her tummy. "I'm going to be a father!" he yelled at the ceiling.

Charlene and Amari congratulated and embraced them.

Derrick whirled with Juna cradled in his arms. As if nothing else mattered, he carried her into their bedroom and set her on the leather sofa in the sitting area.

On his knees, he kissed her, lowered his head to her tummy and whispered, "Mister."

Juna rubbed his head as if she was praying for him. "It might be a girl. I sorry. I know you like boy."

Derrick raised his head. "Boy or girl, I will love the same. But it's a boy because I had a dream."

"You not disappointed if girl?"

"No. Because I know a boy will come. But this baby is a boy."

"I want boy for you."

He smiled and kissed her, then lowered his head to her tummy again. "Mister, your new name is Malachi."

CHAPTER 5

The world was shocked by the news that John Donaldson was elected president. Hidden fear was on the faces of many, but the evangelical leaders on the Far Right hailed him as the chosen one.

While the influential persons on the Left were pointing fingers for the embarrassing loss, the president-elect was at Erich Hornsby's Victorian-style Park Avenue home. The lavish residence filled with antique furnishings, portraits, and artifacts had solid gold toilet seats and tables.

"Congratulations, John, on your victory last night."

"Thank you, Mr. Hornsby. I'm thankful for your prominent support."

"You're very much welcome. At first, we didn't believe your candor would resonate with the voters, but it did. America is ready to return to the days when it was great. You have earned the right to call me, Erich."

"Thank you, Erich. How can I repay you?"

Hornsby reached into the pocket of his red silk smoking jacket and handed him the folded sheet of paper.

The paper rustled as Donaldson unfolded it and read the first two lines. "Are these the people you want me to interview for my cabinet positions?"

"No. Those are the people *for* your cabinet positions. I left the secretary of HUD vacant. You can choose whoever you want for that post."

Donaldson sneered. "I don't want to sound unappreciative, but I have other people in mind for my cabinet positions. I've already taken Colonel Sanders' grandson to be my vice-president. No more!"

"John, this isn't an option. It's an order."

"An order?"

"Yes, an order. I'm the one that organized your campaign. You lost the popular vote by three million but won the electoral college because of my underhandedness."

"And I thank you, but I'm the president now. Sixty-three million people voted for me. I control the party now."

Hornsby calmly replied, "The only thing you control is your mouth. You are the president-elect, but not the president until you are sworn in. And I'm the only guarantee that will happen."

Donaldson stuck out his chest. "Are you threatening me?"

Hornsby remained calm and said, "Not a threat. Just a fact."

"If you have the power you claim, why didn't you stop that nigger from becoming president? He won twice."

"We could've killed him, but it wouldn't've benefited us. We were able to restrict most of his power. Why kill him when he was the perfect recruitment for our cause. He gave rise to someone like you."

Donaldson glanced again at the list. "Was the previous president of the party given a list?"

"Yes. But you are the first to be assigned twenty of the twenty-one positions."

"Why have you tied my hands?"

"Let me be frank. I like you, John. You have the skill to make many believe it's day when it's night. You understand if you make a lie sound like the truth, people will believe it. Your policies and views are the same as mine. Your grandfather and mine attended that 1939 Nazi rally that filled Madison Square Garden. You were taught well by your father. You would be me if you weren't a dotard."

"Dotard? I'm a great businessman and a stable genius!"

"John, you can fool the fools, but not us. A great businessman doesn't become bankrupt six times. A stable genius doesn't misspell common words. I know who you are, Mr. Donaldson. You are a great con artist, but an ignoramus. Your father paid for your college degree. You married your first wife for her money and connections. Your current wife was a high-priced hooker when you met her. You don't have any secrets from us. Enjoy your role as US president. The people we have assigned to your cabinet will make you successful and protect you. We will not stop you from being you, because we are dictators too. Stay on the script, and you will easily get reelected."

Donaldson submissively nodded and looked over the entire list. "So, you're the secretary of state?"

Hornsby stared at him with the answer written in his eyes before he said, "I am every name on that list. Don't mention the names until I give you the go-ahead."

He placed his right hand on Donaldson's left shoulder. "You are the president-elect—no one can take that away. Enjoy yourself; be yourself in front of the media. The people love you—and God has ordained you."

"So why are you in my way if God has ordained me?"

"Because I am God."

* * *

Derrick was on a video call. "Ma, you said Donaldson could win."

"Yeah, but I didn't think he would."

"How could a pathological liar without an empathetic cell in his body, who speaks from the gutter, become president?"

"It's a sign of the times. I'm not saying he is the beast. But he has shown the world how the beast will rise in the earth."

"I think he's the Antichrist. Only the Antichrist would say he has never repented, and only the devil lies about everything."

"Well, he's the president now, and his party controls both chambers of Congress. That increases the importance of our voting initiative. We got two years to make an impact. Let's pray the country doesn't become a totalitarian state before the midterms."

Derrick's brows rose. "We cannot change prophecy. If he's the beast in Revelation, we can't stop him from rising."

Yvonne twisted her closed lips. "He's too stupid to be the beast in Revelation. But I believe he is paving the way."

"You're right. He is too stupid, and his VP looks dumb. So, who is the mastermind?"

"That's the answer we need."

* * *

Nineteen days before the inauguration, Ari Himmelman, the presumed secretary of defense, died from a heart attack. Hornsby immediately summoned an encrypted video call with the council.

"Do we have an alternative?" Samuel Hindenburg asked.

"We do not," Hornsby answered. "His death is a huge blow to our plan."

Daniel Stevens asked, "Can't we move one of our surrogates into that position?"

Hornsby replied, "We have to get the person we select confirmed by the Senate. Most of them in our party will do whatever we say, but there are enough moderates to block the confirmation of the person that I have in mind."

"Where do we go from here? That idiot will probably get impeached in his first year," Stephen Silverton said.

"He is an idiot," Hornsby replied, "but he won't get impeached as long as we maintain control in both chambers. Ari's death is my concern. We only have two of the Joint Chiefs on our ship. We need to identify a new nominee for secretary of defense—someone the moderates in our party will approve. Any suggestions?"

"Get rid of the moderates," Murt Pointer said.

"We will when the time is right," Hornsby replied. "Until then, we need a secretary of defense that won't jump ship when the New Order begins."

"Tom Lynch," Pointer said.

"Tom Lynch? Background?"

"He is the current deputy secretary of defense."

"What! He's in that nigger's administration?" Hornsby said.

"We put him there. He's on our side and can get through the Senate. He can be fired and then replaced with an acting secretary that doesn't need Senate confirmation."

Hornsby grinned. "I love that idea." He paused the call. When he returned, he said, "Meeting adjourned. I have a call from the presidents of Russia and China."

* * *

Brisk weather swept across Suzanne's uncovered face as she trekked on the long narrow path through the frozen snow and entered the small consignment store.

"Hi, Suzanne. Happy New Year! Karen will be right back," the professionally dressed, middle-aged woman behind the glass counter said.

Suzanne was smiling as she took off her black gloves. "Hi, Greta. Thanks. Happy New Year!" She removed her black hooded fit-and-flare coat, placed the gloves inside the pockets, and folded the garment over her left arm.

Dressed in the white turtleneck sweater, fitted blue jeans, and graphite-gray snow boots, Suzanne was browsing the clearance rack when one of the dresses caught her eye. She lifted the dress and laid her coat on the vacant chair outside the fitting room, faced the three-prong mirror, and held the dress against her body.

"That dress will look good on you," one of the four customers said.

Suzanne turned around with her thin lips puckered and twisted. "You think so?"

"Yes. You got the perfect body for it. The colors also enhance your complexion."

"You should work here."

"I would like to if I had the time. But consultant work keeps me traveling. Are you a regular?"

"You can say that. I come here now and then for the sales. I came today to pick up a dress that I ordered. What about you?"

"My first time. I just moved to Boston last week. I'm getting to know the city. Are you picking up a wedding dress?"

"How did you know that?"

"The engagement ring. I like it."

"Thanks."

"When's the wedding?"

"In May."

"Four months. You must be busy."

"I am. I wish I could afford a wedding planner."

"I'm a wedding planner. Well, I used to be one before I broke up with my boyfriend and moved here. I can help you plan the wedding. No charge. It'll be my wedding gift."

"That's very kind of you, but I can't accept. That'll be a burden on you."

"No, it won't. I don't know anyone in Boston. I see it as an opportunity to make new friends and do something I miss."

"You said your consultant work keeps you traveling."

"It does. But I can work on wedding plans in flight and at the hotel. All I need is the internet and a phone."

"Ahm."

"Come on, you'll be doing me a favor. It will be fun."

"Okay."

"What is your name?"

"Suzanne."

The woman extended her hand. "Nice to meet you, Suzanne. I'm Cheryl."

"Hi, Cheryl. This is a coincidence. I was looking for a wedding planner, but they are so expensive, and Leon didn't want us to spend the money."

"I assume Leon is your fiancé."

"He is."

"God knows all of our needs. He sent me to help you. Do you have a venue?"

"Yes. Our church."

"Is that your first choice?"

"Nooo, but it's affordable. We want to spend most of our wedding money on the honeymoon."

"I see. Do you have a caterer?"

"Yes. I'm using RY Caterers. They are very good and affordable."

Suzanne and Cheryl exchanged contact information and communicated daily. The ideas that Cheryl suggested impressed Suzanne and Leon. An extravagant wedding was made affordable.

* * *

When the leaves had returned to the trees and the flowers were blooming, Suzanne and Cheryl were very close friends.

Sobbing as if everything she loved had died, Suzanne phoned Cheryl.

"What happened?" Cheryl worriedly asked.

"I-I s-saw Leon h-having s-sex."

"What? When? Where?"

"On video," she muttered.

"Video? What video? Where did you see the video?"

"It came in my email."

"What? That's crazy. Maybe it's an old tape. Who was the woman?"

Suzanne was wiping the running tears with her fingers. "I don't know, but it wasn't old. He was wearing the watch I bought him for his birthday last month."

"This is crazy. Who would send that video?"

"I think it was her."

"Have you seen her before?"

"No."

"Have you talked to Leon?"

She sniffled and caught her breath. "I sent the video to his cell. He tried to FaceTime, but I didn't want to see him or for him to see me, so I ignored the call. He texted an apology. He said he had a moment of weakness. I gave him a chance to come clean and tell me everything, but he didn't. He said it was only a one-night stand, but I was sent four different videos."

Suzanne's whimpering returned. "W-why did he do this three weeks before the wedding?"

"He doesn't deserve you, Suzanne. Thank God that you found out before you got married. Where are you?"

"Home."

"Where is Leon?"

"I don't know. I told him that I need some time alone. He's been calling, but he hasn't come here."

"I'm more concerned about the person who sent those videos. You need to get out of there. You can stay at my place for a few days. I will come and pick you up."

She sniffled. "Okay."

"Don't answer the door until I get there, and don't accept any calls."

Suzanne mumbled, "Okay."

* * *

After five days at Cheryl's seaport luxury apartment, ignoring the many calls and texts from Leon, Suzanne returned to work and phoned him.

They agreed to meet for lunch at the popular cafe they frequented.

Suzanne arrived early and was sitting in the modern teal two-person booth that faced the entrance. The busy sidewalk and passing vehicles were the view from the bay window at her left. To her right was the circular bar with no empty seats.

Her eyes were focused on the entrance when Leon's dark complexion and Afro fade appeared. Her initial reaction was a happy-to-see-you smile that she quickly removed.

He scooted into the seat facing her. "Hi. I'm sorry, Suzanne. Please forgive me. I love you."

Her closed hands were on the table, and he tried to hold them, but she pulled away.

"Say something," he said.

She slid her closed left hand on the table and opened it.

"Please put that ring back on. I don't want it back, and I don't believe you want to give it back. I'm sorry about what I did. I don't love her. It was only sex. She doesn't mean anything to me."

Suzanne frowned. The corner of one lip went back and forth before she forced a closed-mouth smile. "Take your ring back, Leon. The feeling is gone, and it's not coming back. There is nothing you can say or do to change that."

He stared with shame written on his face. Tears formed in his eyes.

Suzanne lifted the ring from the palm of her hand and set it on the table. She said, "Goodbye, Leon," and headed toward the exit and didn't look back.

The next day when Suzanne arrived home from work, she sat on the regal blue twill sofa, a bowl of pineapple sherbet in one hand and the television remote in the other.

"BREAKING NEWS" scrolled across the bottom screen. *"Famed former hedge fund manager, Arthur Kornish, was found hanging in his cell. Attempts to resuscitate him failed. Mr. Kornish was in the second week of his nine-month sentence for lying to the FBI about the murder-suicide of Ryan Mendendorf and his family. Mr. Mendendorf was the CEO of Third Eye Films, the company owned by the controversial Derrick Williams, who is under federal investigation..."*

Suzanne paused with her mouth open. *Derrick is under federal investigation?*

* * *

A year later, Suzanne and Cheryl were at the Boston waterfront bar in the festive atmosphere of Cinco de Mayo. The tune by Baby Bash was playing in the background.

"Let's go to Miami for a vacation. Have you been to Miami?"

"I haven't," Suzanne said with the mojito lifted toward her mouth and her body swaying to the music.

"Let's go. South Beach is great. We can also go to the grand opening of the community built by that guy who made the Adam and Eve movie."

"Derrick Williams?"

"Yeah, that's him."

"I know him."

"You know him?"

"We dated in college."

"You dated him? He is so fine. How did you let him get away?"

"It was just one of those things."

"I bet you still have feelings for him, huh?"

"He's married."

"Uh-huh, you still have feelings."

"I don't."

"Yes, you do. If you didn't, you wouldn't've answered the way you did."

Suzanne paused in thought before she said, "I heard he was under federal investigation."

"I heard that too, but it's bogus. The white man is always trying to keep a successful black man down. They didn't find anything because he's having the grand opening for his community. So, you want to go? I can see it in your face that you do."

"How long are we going to stay?"

"A week. We can go down to the Keys and hop over to the Bahamas after the opening."

"We probably won't get to see him."

Cheryl cracked a smile. "Yes, we will. I have front row tickets to the concert and an invite to the afterparty."

"How did you get that?"

"I'm a marketing consultant. You know how us black women roll. We can get what we want when we want it."

Suzanne smiled. *It would be nice to see him again.* "When is it?"

"Next month."

"That's too soon. My supervisor might not approve."

"Yes, he will. Ask him."

"What makes you so confident that he will approve my leave? What do you know that I don't?"

"I know he likes you. That's all I need to know. I saw how he looked at you at the office Christmas party. He wished you were under the mistletoe."

Suzanne grinned.

CHAPTER 6

The federal investigation into Third Eye Films had closed without any indictments.

Juna had given birth to Malachi and was five months pregnant when Derrick, Obe, and Gladys flew to Miami in preparation for the grand opening.

During the private three-hour flight, Xavier and Gladys watched a video while Derrick was video chatting with Juna. When the conversation ended, he joined them.

"What is this?" he asked.

"It's our Passover," Xavier said.

"That's the uniform for Passover?"

"We don't wear it to celebrate Passover. It's our uniform during the fall, winter, and spring months. You saw us in our summer uniform."

Derrick was intently listening to the sermon by one of the many ministers on the pulpit. The nearly bald and distinguished-looking elderly man wore glasses. Pinned on his extra-long, plain dark-brown suit was a heart-shaped rosette that dangled four colored ribbons. An ivory-silk vest covered his white tuxedo-style shirt with a bow tie that matched the suit.

"Who is he?" Derrick asked.

"Bishop Stallings," Xavier replied.

"Where is he from?"

"New Haven, Connecticut."

"Connecticut? You have a church in Connecticut?"

"Yes, we do."

"He's a great man. I'd like to meet him."

"I can arrange that."

"Looking forward to it. On another note, President Donaldson is becoming more dangerous because Congress is allowing him to get away with obvious violations of the law."

"That's because the alt-right is the majority in the House and Senate," Gladys said. "But your mother's plan for the midterms is working. According to the polls that I've seen, the Left is on track to win the House, and the Senate is a toss-up."

"Without both, he can't be stopped. I can see the Left regaining the majority in the House, but by how much? Looking at the states in play, I don't think they can win the Senate. Another problem is the far-right evangelicals. They continue to support Donaldson's injurious policies and blatant lies."

"A lot of people took a chance and voted for Donaldson," Gladys said. "But anyone who still supports him is either a fool or a racist."

Derrick tilted his head. "A lot of white evangelicals voted twice for the black president. They aren't racists."

"No, they're not. But if they voted for Donaldson and still support him, what does that make them? We are living in dangerous times. In the eyes of the religious alt-right, Donaldson is the chosen one to bring back the Germanic Aryan nation, the symbol of the blond-haired German."

"If we can vote his allies out of office, we will remove his power. The million-dollar question is, how do we get the lazies to vote? If a maniac like Donaldson doesn't motivate them, what and who will?"

"Your mother," Gladys said.

* * *

On the third Saturday in June, at noon Derrick stood at the podium in front of the newly built community center. An estimated crowd that exceeded two hundred thousand faced him.

"On behalf of the Unity Corporation and its investors, I welcome everyone to the grand opening of all four phases of the Black Economic Empowerment Community.

"I thank God, my wife, my mother, my sister, my brothers Mister and Junior, who are watching from heaven, and my father, Cedric Williams, who is watching with them.

"Special recognition goes to Xavier Greene, the Chief Operating Officer, to Gladys Greene, the Executive Vice-President, and to all Unity Corporation investors and staff."

After Derrick had read the names of each investor and staff member, he said, "If you are wondering why we decided to wait until all four phases were completed before we held the grand opening, the suggestion came from my mother, Yvonne Dunbar. She said the opening would have a greater impact if we waited until the completion of all four phases. She was right—look at the crowd. Today is the beginning of greater things to come, and I want to thank the homeowners and retailers for their patience.

"I also want to make it clear the Unity Corporation projects do not promote segregation. But if we do not look out for own people, who will? We exist to be the helping hand for black people to gain quality education, employment, business opportunity, business and personal loans, and to save money on retail and gas prices.

"Instead of hoping that others will have the heart to help us, we have put ourselves in the position where we can help ourselves and others because that is the government of God."

Rousing applause erupted among the diverse crowd.

Derrick waited until the claps and cheers subsided. "There are many in high places claiming to love God. But how can you love God when you turn away those who come to your borders in search of salvation? How can you love God when you approve cruelty on children? How can you love God when you are a pathological liar?"

More applause with agreeing shouts halted his words before he continued.

"We need everyone to vote. There is a devil in the White House, and Congress is not keeping him in check. We need a new Congress that will hold him accountable. Make sure you vote in November and encourage others to vote. Because if the current party continues as the majority in both chambers of Congress, America will become Nazi Germany.

"But we the people hold political power in our hand. We have to use that power. We have to vote!

"I'm one of the many who took it for granted that Donaldson wouldn't win and didn't vote. So, I'm guilty of allowing the devil to enter the White House—and everyone who didn't vote is also guilty."

A male voice in the crowd shouted, "What about those who voted for John Donaldson?"

Derrick's eyes scanned in the direction. He paused on a few faces as his tongue twisted side to side in his mouth. "To answer that question, I say this: Many took a chance and voted for Donaldson. But as the wise woman told me, if you still support the president after all that he has said and done, you are either a racist or a fool."

Derrick paused until the rousing applause and cheers subsided.

"Please add your email address to our mailing list. An hour from now, we will randomly select one hundred people who registered their email addresses. Each person will receive four tickets for tonight's concert at the amphitheater. You can register your email at the welcome center inside the facility behind me. We didn't expect such a large crowd, but we have ordered more food. There will be enough for everyone. Again, thank you for your support!"

After the heads of the Unity Corporation and the attending investors cut the ribbon in front of the community center, the doors to all four phases opened. Free shuttle rides circled the community. Booths serving free hot dogs, hamburgers, popcorn, and drinks were in multiple places. Clowns, carnival-style rides, and local musical talent provided entertainment for the festive event that ended at 4:00 p.m.

* * *

Lustful looks followed Suzanne and Cheryl as they strolled a mile in both directions on the South Beach sand at the aqua water's edge. Suzanne was wearing the light blue bralette bikini top set. Her triangular bottom had a skimpy fit that stretched upward. Cheryl wore the white bikini set. Her mesh top had sun floral appliqué. The bottom was a skimpy low rise.

"What are you thinking about?" Cheryl asked as the warm water splashed across her feet.

"I'm not thinking about anything," Suzanne said, distracted.

"Yes, you are. You're thinking about Derrick."

"I'm not thinking about him. He's married."

"Mm-hmm. You're thinking about him. We will see him tonight."

"I'm not thinking about him. Let's talk about something else."

Cheryl cast a sideways smile. "It's almost four. Let's go eat."

* * *

After they had eaten and shrugged the fifth invitation of the day from men who perceived them to be wantons, they returned to their hotel rooms on Collins Avenue and prepared for the 8:00 p.m. concert.

Suzanne was rocking the white, fitted mock neck sweater dress and four-inch black heels with a black leather hand purse.

Cheryl wore the black bandage strappy dress that covered her nipples but exposed half of her round breasts. Her four-inch heels were leopard skin that matched her purse.

Eyes watched as the VIP attendant at the amphitheater escorted them down the steps to the second-row middle seats.

"This place is beautiful," Suzanne said.

Bright-eyed, Cheryl squeezed next to her. "I love it. Look at the stars in the sky—so beautiful."

Suzanne looked but then scanned for Derrick.

From the opening act with YBN Nahmir & YBN Almighty Jay through the John Legend closing act, Suzanne continued to look for Derrick.

At the end of the concert, she turned to Cheryl, who was applauding the encore performance by John Legend. "We should've come to the ribbon cutting. He probably went back home after the opening ceremony."

Cheryl, with her eyes on John Legend, said, "He will be at the afterparty."

"How do you know?"

When John Legend left the stage, Cheryl faced her. "Trust me. This is a very big day for him. He has to celebrate with the investors. No one comes to Miami and leaves without partying."

Suzanne nodded and continued to look for Derrick even as they rode from the property in the taxi.

* * *

The Art Deco district led to the estate of Mr. Davis, one of the chief investors for the Unity Corporation. Cheryl excitedly led Suzanne by the hand as they exited the vehicle and presented their invitation to one of the five armed guards that blocked the entrance.

They entered the home and stepped on inlaid marble that led to leather flooring in an open space illuminated by multiple crystal chandeliers.

"He's here," Cheryl whispered.

"I'm not looking for him. He's married." *Where is he?*

"From what you told me, he is still in love with you. If he doesn't know it yet, he will when he sees you."

This ain't right. I don't want to be with a married man. "Cheryl, let's go."

"Go! We just got here. Let's party a little."

"I feel guilty."

"Okay, forget about Derrick. Look at all these fine men. You might meet your soulmate."

Suzanne relaxed. "There are a lot of handsome men here."

"Yesss. We are in the single woman's paradise surrounded by men that are debonair, rich, handsome, and black. Hmm. I might find my husband here."

Suzanne half-smiled.

Several men approached. Cheryl flirted with each one. But Suzanne was only polite. Her eyes kept searching for Derrick.

* * *

Dressed in his usual dapperness, Derrick was in the private room on FaceTime. After the conversation with Juna, he entered the space where the guests had assembled. Investors who weren't at the ceremony quickly approached him.

He was conversing when he noticed a woman that looked like Suzanne. They made eye contact. He smiled; she smiled.

"Suzanne!" he yelled and rushed toward her.

Cheryl walked away as if she wasn't with her.

"Hi, what are you doing here?" he asked, smiling.

Suzanne was speechless, seemingly unsure of what to say. Her eyes glistened as if she was looking at her teen idol.

"How did you get here?" he asked.

"Ahm, I came with a friend."

"Where is he?"

"It's a she."

"O-okay. Where is she?"

"I think she wanted us to talk alone."

"I see. You look stunning as usual. How have you been?"

"Okay. Can't complain. I see you're married now."

"I am. Have you met your soulmate?"

"I thought I had, but he cheated on me a few weeks before the wedding."

"What? That doesn't make sense."

"I think he met a fatal attraction."

"What makes you think that?"

"I was sent videos of their sexual trysts."

"Videos? I'm sorry you had to experience that. But I'm glad to see you. I've been waiting for years to apologize. At the time, I didn't realize that I was you scaring you away."

"Yes, you did."

"I'm sorry. I only wanted to apologize. But everything happens for a reason. I was hoping you would've tried to contact me over the years, but I guess I broke a heart that couldn't be mended for me."

"It wasn't that. I felt like you were stalking me, so I hid. I saw your Adam and Eve movie but thought you had moved on. That's when I met and fell in love with Leon."

"You know I don't believe in coincidences. So how did you get here? Are you living in Miami now?"

"No, Boston."

"Boston! What brought you here?"

"My friend Cheryl suggested we vacation in Miami and come to the community opening."

"But how did you make it to this party? Only investors and their guests have invitations."

"Cheryl said a friend gave her an invite."

"Who's the friend?"

"I don't know. I didn't ask."

"How long have you and her been friends?"

"Almost two years."

"Where did you meet?"

"Why do I feel like you're interrogating me?"

"You know how I like to ask questions. Just curious about how God made our paths cross again."

"We met shopping. I mentioned that I was getting married but couldn't afford a wedding planner, and she volunteered her services."

"She's a wedding planner?"

"She did it part-time before she moved to Boston after the breakup with her boyfriend. She works as a marketing consultant. I think that's how she got the invite."

"Where is she? I'd like to meet her."

Suzanne turned to look around the open space.

When Derrick saw her petite rounded rear that pushed against the tight dress, he felt an urge.

She turned and faced him. "I don't see her."

"I'm sure I'll get to meet her before you leave. Let me introduce you to some friends."

Suzanne followed him to the woman in full Afro-centric garb.

"Gladys, this is Suzanne."

"Is this the Suzanne that I've heard so much about?"

"Yes, it is."

"It's a small world," Gladys said with her eyes locked into Derrick's.

"Have you seen my mother?" he asked.

"She flew back to Philadelphia with Amari and Charlene after the concert. Can we talk in private for a minute?"

"Sure." He faced Suzanne. "I'll be right back."

Derrick and Gladys entered the room where he had chatted with Juna.

With an intense expression, Gladys immediately said, "How did she get here?"

"I know where you're going. But I'm sure she doesn't know that she's being used."

"What makes you so sure?"

"A few weeks before her marriage, she was sent recent videos of her fiancé having sex with a woman. The person of interest is the woman that brought her here. One of our investors gave her an invite. We have a mole in our group."

"We will deal with that later. Right now, what are you going to do about Suzanne? Do you still have feelings for her?"

"Not as much as I thought I would. I'm surprised."

"I'm glad to hear that. You have a beautiful wife who loves you more than herself. Don't spoil it."

"I won't."

"They were betting that you still had feelings for Suzanne and would spend the night with her. I'm sure the plan was to get you to go to a place where a secret camera is in place to record you. She is the pawn to lose your clergy support."

"Well, it won't work. The only woman I'm getting in bed with is my wife."

When Derrick stepped out of the room, with Gladys closely behind, a woman was standing next to Suzanne, and two seemingly zealous men faced them.

Suzanne, who was periodically looking over the man's shoulder, locked her eyes on Derrick when she saw him.

Cheryl noticed Derrick and politely pushed through the two men with Suzanne at her side. With a hefty smile, he approached them, and Suzanne introduced Cheryl.

He extended his hand. "Hi, nice to meet you. Suzanne told me that a friend of yours gave you an invite."

"Yeah. I hope it's okay."

"Of course. Beautiful women always have a place at the party. What's your friend's name? I want to thank him or her."

"Thank him?" Cheryl said.

"Yes. I wouldn't have seen Suzanne without him."

She chuckled. "Daryl Dennison."

"Oh, Daryl. I haven't seen him tonight. If you don't mind me asking, how do you know Daryl?"

"Is there something wrong? You are asking a lot of questions."

"I'm sorry. Suzanne can tell you that I'm always asking questions."

Suzanne interjected, "He's always been that way since the first day I met him."

"I'm a consultant for his company," Cheryl said.

"Suzanne said that you are a marketing consultant. Maybe you can do some work for me? Are you interested?"

She broadened her smile. "I'm always interested in new clients."

"Great."

The three-way chat continued for several minutes while most of the guests were watching the Eddie Henderson hologram performance.

"You guys look cute together," Cheryl said. "I'm going to give y'all some private time."

"Don't leave."

"Two is company and three is a crowd." With her eyes intently fixed on his, Cheryl said, "I like crowds in private places. Maybe we can party together later. But I know you haven't seen each other in years, so I'll let the two of you have some private time."

Derrick smiled. "I asked you not to leave because I have to go." He noted the disappointment on Suzanne's face.

"Don't leave, Derrick," Cheryl said. "Let's go to Jet Blue. Suzanne told me that you love to dance."

"I can't. I have a plane to catch."

"This time of night?"

"Yeah, I need to go home to my wife. I miss her."

Suzanne lowered her eyes, and Derrick could see the defeat in Cheryl's expression.

"It was good to see you again, Suzanne. I pray you will find the happiness you deserve." He leaned forward, placed his lips against her soft cheek, and whispered in her ear. "Do you trust me?"

"Yes," she said openly.

He continued to whisper, "Don't say a word. Keep smiling like I'm flirting. Some people are trying to ruin my life. They know how much I love you and are trying to use you as a pawn. If Cheryl disappears from your life when you return to Boston, know that she had something to do with the breakup between you and your fiancé. I still love you; I always will. But I'm in love with someone else."

His mouth lifted from her ear. "I wrote a poem about you."

"Recite it, please," Cheryl said with excitement. "I want to hear it."

He gazed into Suzanne's saddened eyes and said:
"She is the beauty of an ancient Egyptian queen
With eyes so sensuous, seductive, and green.
And here I sit, far from her side
Wondering if in her heart I still abide.
For years have passed since I last saw her face,
So have all memories of me been erased.
Are my hopes a false dream,
Or will our love again be seen?
Those are the questions I wonder about,
But in my heart I have no doubt.
That Suzanne one day
Will come back this way."

Tears slid down Suzanne's smile.

Cheryl said, "That was so beautiful. I'm going to let you two have a private moment."

Derrick shifted his eyes to Cheryl. "Don't leave. I want you to hear this."

He faced Suzanne. "My poem is prophecy fulfilled. You came back this way."

She wiped her tears. "I did, but our love isn't seen again."

"It's been seen again. We're looking at it. But there is a greater love than the love we had. I found it in my wife. Don't get married until you find that love too. Goodbye, Suzanne."

He turned and walked away without looking back.

* * *

Suzanne's watering eyes followed his every step until he disappeared among the bodies.

Cheryl snarled and turned to her. "Let's go."

Suzanne didn't respond.

"Suzanne."

In the feelings of what could've been, her fingers wiped away the tears. She faced Cheryl with a forced smile. "Okay, let's go."

Unable to sleep because of the mixed thoughts that pounded the forefront of her mind, Suzanne rose in red, lacy, string-bikini panties and matching bra, wrapped herself with the hotel's white terry-cloth robe, and sat barefoot on the room's balcony. The sound of the ocean's waves landing on the golden sand brought solace.

Time seemingly passed unnoticed as the sun lifted to the water's edge, and the birds chirped. Torn between Derrick's words and her own belief, Suzanne phoned Cheryl's room. The unanswered call surprised her. She immediately phoned Cheryl's cell, but the call went to voicemail. Was Derrick right about Cheryl? But then she had the thought that *maybe she hooked up with one of those guys at the party* and believed it.

Bored, she opened her social media accounts and read messages, responding to some. She took selfies with the pink sky as the background. "Everything but the Girl" was the music from her cell as she watched the low tide.

The early visitors to the beach were a welcome sight. She was smiling at the liveliness while waiting for the scheduled 8:00 a.m. breakfast with Cheryl.

At 8:03 a.m. she phoned Cheryl's cell, but the call went to voicemail again. She phoned the room, but after five rings hung up. *Maybe she's in the shower.*

With mixed thoughts, Suzanne walked barefoot in the robe to Cheryl's room, a few doors down from hers, and saw the housekeeper's cart at the open door.

She peeked inside.

"Can I help you?" the Spanish accent asked.

"This is my friend's room. Do you know where she is?"

"Person check out."

Suzanne went back to her room, dazed. She flopped face-first on the bed and cried—in agony because she was deceived, in heartache because she was still in love with Derrick.

CHAPTER 7

In the backseat of the SUV headed to the airport, Derrick, Xavier, and Gladys were discussing the mole.

"We have the right to terminate an investor without cause," Gladys said. "But we have to return their investment and compensate for the amount earned."

"That's not a problem. Do it." Derrick replied.

Xavier interjected, "We need to do more than that!"

"Like what?"

"Like adding his name to Sambo's Cabin. That page has six million followers. Folks start hiding when they become pinned on that page."

"My mother posts those names to put the sellout politicians and sycophants on blast."

"Isn't he a sycophant?"

"Yeah, he is." Derrick nodded twice with his lips puckered. "I'll ask my mother to add his name."

Gladys said, "I already texted her, and she replied, YES!"

"When did you text her?"

"When we learned about Daryl."

He nodded.

"By the way, why did your mother name the page Sambo's Cabin and not Uncle Tom's?" Xavier asked.

"I asked the same question and she educated me. Uncle Tom was a house slave that was helping the field slaves. He was looking out for them in every way. That's why the slaves called him Uncle, an endearment name. But whitey changed it, so we would use the term to degrade the person that should be respected. The Sambo image is the house Negro."

Gladys said, "You should make a movie about the real Uncle Tom."

Derrick's brows lifted. "You're right. I will."

***

"BREAKING NEWS" scrolled across the bottom of the television screen: *"MLS star, Roberto Cinteron, was killed in a single-car accident. His wife survived the crash without injury."*

Yvonne's brows raised and her eyes widened, mouth frozen open, a facial expression that remained for a few seconds before she said, "Vengeance is mine saith the LORD!"

The portal rang, and she answered.

"Ma, you heard about Roberto?" Derrick said.

"I heard. Now you know why I told the family to let the Lord handle it."

Derrick paused before he said, "Yes. I can rest now."

She raised her voice, "You can rest now? You should've been able to rest by trusting the Lord would avenge in due time. I have rest because of my faith and trust in the Lord. That is how I dealt with the pain of your father's death, and stepfather, and Mister, and Junior. That is how I kept my head from going under the troubled waters that existed before Mister was born."

Derrick's eyes lowered for a second. "You're right. Let's talk about the future. How is your project going?"

Yvonne perked up. "The commercials that Blue made are a big hit. We have over a million teens signed up as volunteers."

"Wow! How many of them can vote in the midterms?"

"823,000 as of today."

"823,000? That's awesome. Hopefully, we will win the House."

"I'm confident that we will win big in the House, but the Senate will be close."

"I'm not expecting a win there because of the demographics. But you think you can help the Left win big in the House?"

"Yes."

"You will have to win some of those gerrymandering districts."

"We will. Quelle has put together a very strong nationwide strategic plan."

"You got a lot of confidence in that young guy."

"We are going to win the Senate seat in Alabama because of him."

"Alabama? Ma, I think that's asking too much. Those confederates in Alabama don't care if their candidate is a pedophile. He's one of them."

"I believe there are enough who care. They might not vote for our candidate, but they won't vote for theirs either. That's a win for us because Quelle has organized a strong turnout of black women for this election."

"What is he, a ladies' man?"

"He's a young black man who cares about his state—and black and white voters can appreciate that."

"Where did you find him?"

"He's a graduate from one of the HBCUs."

"You have hired a lot of them."

"Because that is where most of our greatest minds are."

"I agree. How is Cynthia?"

"Her cancer is in full remission."

"Wow! Praise God! Partial remission or complete remission?"

"I said full remission. That's complete remission."

"What's wrong? You sound a little huffy. I just wanted to be clear."

"I was clear, but you insulted my intelligence."

"How did I do that?"

"I said her cancer is in full remission. Why did you imply that I might've meant partial? Full means full, and partial means not full."

"I apologize."

"Apology accepted."

"I'm happy for Cynthia. The doctors said her cancer wouldn't change. I was just surprised to hear that it went into full remission."

"You see how God works? Do you see the power of prayer? You need to start going to church. God is sending you messages. He's telling you to go to church. Your wife has stopped going to Mass because of you. You need to find a church, Derrick. You need the fellowship that is there."

"I'm going to join Amari's church," he said.

"Good. I like the spirit in that church. I'll go with you sometimes. When are you joining?"

"This Saturday."

"Is Juna joining too?"

"I told her that she doesn't have to, but she said she wants to go with me. So, I'll go with her to Mass."

Yvonne smiled. "I like that."

"I got the better of the deal—Mass is only an hour—but you know Amari's churches are all-day."

Yvonne chuckled. "But the church isn't boring. I can stay all day."

Derrick smiled and said, "How does a man who didn't like going to church for an hour, be comfortable in church all day?"

"When he's led by the Holy Ghost."

* * *

Minister Kabir honored Derrick's urgent request to meet. When Derrick entered the North African-inspired home, he faced the large gold-framed picture of Elijah Muhammad and nodded.

With one escort in front and another behind, he stepped onto the hardwood floors and followed the path of the Arabian rugs.

He walked through the arched white-marbled walls and entered the living area where the Minister sat stalwartly at the cherrywood table.

"It is an honor to meet you, sir," Derrick said with an extended hand before he sat on the cushioned matching chair at the other end of the six-foot table.

"Peace be with you," Kabir said in Arabic. "I've only heard good things about you, Mr. Williams. How can I serve you?"

"Thank you, sir. The Unity Corporation has endorsed five Muslim candidates for the House of Representatives and one for the US Senate. I need your support behind all of our candidates. President Donaldson, as you know, is a very dangerous man. He reminds me of how Adolf Hitler came to power and overthrew the German democracy. What concerns me the most is how Congress is allowing him to disregard the Constitution. We have to gain control of Congress to keep him in check until the next presidential election."

Minister Kabir removed his thin eyeglasses and held them in his right hand. The white around his dark brown eyes widened. "I supported the black president both times. I'm willing to support blacks that I believe won't sell us out. That's one of the reasons why I admire your mother. She has black candidates that I can support. But I'm not willing to support the white candidates that she endorses, the same as you don't allow white investors."

Derrick cupped his hands on the table and leaned forward on his elbows. "Minister Kabir, I don't allow white investors, but white people can live and operate a business on our properties. I believe God will judge every person by their heart and not their race. We trust the black and white candidates that we support—not because of their words—but their actions.

"The election and reelection of the black president was a phenomenon that occurred because Blacks, Whites, Latinos, Asians, Arabs, Jews, and Indians voted for him. That was a sign of political power that we didn't harness.

"While we were satisfied with having a black man in the Oval Office, we lost focus on the big picture. We didn't realize the importance of maintaining both chambers of Congress. We didn't realize how much hate was in the underbelly of America because a black man was elected president. And when he got reelected, that hate removed its mask. That opened the path for someone like Donaldson to rise and become president.

"The alt-right feels empowered because of him. They are energized and motivated to maintain political control. We cannot allow that to happen. They want me dead, and all I'm doing is trying to economically empower black people to remove them from the welfare and unemployment lines. How much more do they want to kill you when you inspire millions spiritually like Dr. Martin Luther King? I'm sure you realize the level of fear that you put in them when you were able to gather over a million black men in one place. They saw an army. You are a bigger threat than me. If you were a Christian, you might've been dead by now. United, we can change America until Judgment Day."

* * *

While Derrick was imploring support from those on the outskirts of political interest, Yvonne was traveling across the country to meet in person with her staff on the campaign trails.

Thirty days before the midterms, she was in Alabama to meet with Quelle Curtis, the twenty-four-year-old political science graduate from Alabama State University.

"What are we looking like on the ground?" she asked.

"I'm still confident that we can win Alabama," he said.

"Even with Donaldson holding rallies?"

"Yes. I've been working in the counties where Donaldson is very popular. They love him but are hesitant to vote for the candidate he supports. Like I said, if I can lower the margin of victory in those counties, we can win the state with a strong turnout from the inner-cities and suburbs."

"Quelle, if you can pull this off, not only will your raise be significant, but the bonus too."

He smiled and ran his hand across his temple-fade haircut. "I don't do this for the money. I'm doing it for the cause."

"I know. Count the reward as a gift from God."

His lips curled. "Black women from the inner cities and white women in the suburbs will win Alabama for our candidate."

"I like your confidence."

"I'm very confident. My ears are on the ground in this state—and the ground is saying that a lot of people in those rural counties will not vote."

"What about the state legislatures?"

"No chance. This is Alabama. They love the color red. But when our candidate wins the Senate, he might be able to convert enough during his term to turn the state purple."

"Quelle, that alone is victory."

CHAPTER 8

Concerned about his party's deficit in the polls, Hornsby ordered Donaldson to declare a state of emergency on the caravan of immigrants that was traveling from Central America for asylum in the USA. He labeled them as rapists, drug dealers, and murderers. Those criminals were added by Hornsby's hand, who paid them to make the caravan appear as a threat. Troops were sent to the border to influence fear among the American people that they might believe the politicians on the Right were their only protectors and keep the Right in control of Congress.

Every day up to election morning, the president and XOF news aired the caravan as invaders who were going to illegally enter into America and increase crime because the Left had blocked the wall from being built. But on the morning after the midterm elections, Hornsby had an encrypted video call with the council members.

"Last night, we suffered a major setback. We allowed the liberals to gain leadership in both chambers of Congress! Their victory in the House is so big, they can have thirty defectors and still have enough votes to impeach the president."

"But they only have a two-vote advantage in the Senate," Technology billionaire Murt Pointer said. "They still cannot convict him."

"Yes, we will survive in the Senate. But they won Alabama! Alabama! If they can win Alabama, they can win the South!"

"But we had a flawed candidate in Alabama."

"Even a flawed candidate should win Alabama!"

"Where do we go from here?" General Haldeman, the chairman of the Joint Chiefs of Staff, asked.

Hornsby gave a hateful frown. "That Italian bitch will become Speaker of the House again. She won't visit Camp David with Donaldson and the VP. She's too smart. So, we go to plan B."

"What's plan B? You haven't told us," Jake Getz asked.

"Donaldson's reelection. We commissioned hypothetical polls last month. Donaldson and Hornsby are within the margin of error against the Left's leading candidate. That's six points better. I'm replacing the VP on the ticket. We have lost the House and don't have control of the Pentagon, a conundrum caused because Donaldson keeps going off script. The idiot doesn't know how to keep his mouth shut. When we win reelection, we will eliminate him and proceed with the plan."

"What if we lose?" Jake asked.

"If we lose the election, we will start the civil war."

"Williams is in the way. He has met more than once with Minister Kabir," Murt said.

"I knew he would continue to be a problem," Hornsby said. "The lucky son of a bitch has escaped twice. Not only is he in the way, he has cut into my profits."

"So, when are we going to remove him from the earth?" Samuel asked. "Our customers are patronizing his businesses. A white man in Montana and a white woman in Iowa are two managers of his superstores that sell only black products. Can you believe that? White people are buying sodas made by niggers."

Hornby nodded. "We have to remove him, but we can't afford to bring suspicion on the far right. Let him become a victim of black-on-black crime. Black lives only matter when the white man kills a nigger, so let a nigger kill a nigger. They are doing it every day. If there weren't so many of them, they would be extinct by now. That shows how well we have programmed them. We even got them calling each other niggers—and their women, hoes and bitches. Dumb-ass niggers."

* * *

When the new members of Congress were sworn in, the Unity Corporation had opened its bank, the four phases in Miami were thriving, and economically empowered black communities had risen across the country.

At one dollar per gallon less, Unity Corporation petroleum was the gas of choice. Motorists within fifty miles of the stations were regular customers. The televisions at the pumps were advertising the products, stores, and the Third Eye films and cable channels.

Charter schools that offered vocational and college prep courses were in Miami, D.C., Detroit, Atlanta, Chicago, New York, New Orleans, Compton, and in cities in North and South Carolina, Mississippi, Georgia, and Alabama.

The Unity Corporation had also purchased one of the major theater chains that added to their chain of independent theaters, and Third Eye Films released *Hannibal* and *Deadwood Dick* exclusively at those theaters. Both were worldwide blockbusters.

Ruth was operating her bakery in the Piedmont Triad, with franchises in every Unity Corporation community. Beverly, Ruben, and Steve worked at the North Carolina stores. Diane owned the store in Miami. Phyllis owned the store in Atlanta. Stephanie owned the store in Detroit.

Charlene had finished medical school, with her residency in Philadelphia. She and Amari were engaged.

Juna had given birth to her second child, Rhea-Toni, and was pregnant again. Her mother, Emy, had a green card and was living at the penthouse.

* * *

As uninvited guests, Derrick and Gladys went to Davos, Switzerland, to interact with attendees at the World Economic Forum. They had the savvy to network after business hours at the high-end restaurants, bars, and lounges, which led them to attend an exclusive party up in the mountains.

Inside the private chalet that featured a stone fireplace and ten-person Jacuzzi on the first floor of the open space, the ceiling speakers played the low-volume music of Jocelyn Pook.

In Afro-centric garb, Gladys was networking with the African business elite. Derrick was on the other side of the well-lit space, networking with European and Asian chief executives when he saw Erich Hornsby in conversation with the familiar Russian oligarch. He stared at the two men, whose backs were to him, before his attention returned to the business conversation at hand.

Moments later, one of the topless women in the Jacuzzi, stepped out in her black thong and took the hand of the Russian oligarch. She led him upstairs to one of the seven bedrooms.

Hornsby stepped closer to the open window and appeared to be in thought as he stared at the snow-covered trees.

Derrick approached. "Hello, Mr. Hornsby."

He quickly turned around, surprised. "How did you get in here?"

"God paved the way."

"God? I am God!"

Derrick didn't flinch, but Hornsby's raised voice turned heads.

Derrick smiled to distract the attention drawn to them, then he said softly, "Jesus answered them, 'Is it not written in your law, I said, Ye are gods? If he called them gods, unto whom the word of God came, and the Scripture cannot be broken." (St. John 10:34-35)

Hornsby stared.

Derrick said, "According to those Scriptures, I am a god. But I am not God; neither are you."

"Mr. Williams, you are a smart nigger but still a nigger."

"Mr. Hornsby, the reason for using that disparaging word is because you hate the man that gave birth to all human life. You hate your father."

"My father?" Hornsby chuckled. "Listen, boy, we have allocated your slice of the minority pie. But you want a slice of our pie. That is something you cannot have. Be a good nigger and buy a professional sports team, or start your own clothing line, or produce some rap music, or be content with your cable channels and film company. You don't belong here. You are out of your league. I'm hosting a workshop next month on the State Department's grant opportunities for minority businesses—that is where you belong."

"And my hand will be at that workshop because I grab low-hanging fruit for those who can't reach it. Regarding your continuous use of disparaging words, there are words that I can call you. And unlike yours, mine are true. I don't want a slice of your pie because I am baking my own, and you know that it will be much better than yours. That is why you are trying to stop me. But you can't. That is why God has put me in this room with you—to remind you that you can't. Your pie is done, and I am already cutting into your profits. Your fear is when my pie comes out of the oven."

"I have no fear, Mr. Williams. I bring fear to others." He patted Derrick on the upper arm. "Stay safe," he said as he walked away.

Derrick turned and watched with a smile before his eyes shifted in the direction of Gladys, who was smiling back at him. He stepped around the stationary people, some of whom held drinks, and joined Gladys. After he shared the conversation with Hornsby, the two mingled with the Nigerian president before they left the chalet.

* * *

As the days in America continued in political turmoil, Yvonne represented Derrick at the State Department workshop. She was strolling along the hotel's reception hall, unfamiliar with anyone, but the eyes of many were on her.

Yvonne had risen to prominence from her grassroots efforts that contributed to the Left becoming the majority in both chambers of Congress. Some looked at her with admiration, some with jealousy, others with hate. She felt the variation of the looks as she moved in the navy-blue chiffon cape gown with her natural, graceful presence that attracted the unmarried and married.

"Mrs. Dunbar," came from a friendly voice behind her.

She turned, anticipating it was someone she had met before. When she saw Erich Hornsby there, she hesitated before she pleasantly said, "Yes."

He extended his hand. "My name is Erich Hornsby."

She shook his hand. "I know who you are. How do you know me?"

"I have to know you. You're the reason we lost control of Congress."

"I'm not the reason. The president's policies and corruption are the reasons."

"The people don't care about policies and corruption. That's something they complain about in public. But when they enter the voting booth, their worry is illegal immigrants and the crime around them."

"If that is true, why is his approval rating at 40 percent?"

"His approval on the economy is over 60 percent. That will win his reelection. The voters know a poor economy means more crime. The most important thing for people is to wake up the next morning. Safety influences their vote."

"That didn't work in the midterm."

"We didn't emphasize it enough."

Yvonne lowered her brows and gave him a neutral stare.

"I see the contempt and disgust on your face, Mrs. Dunbar. I can explain myself better in a private conversation. Care to join me?"

"Sure."

Followed by his three-person security team, Hornsby walked at Yvonne's side. "You are a very impressive black woman."

"I'm a very impressive woman, Mr. Hornsby, whether black or white."

"You are overly sensitive, like most women. Are you having a blood day?"

Yvonne halted. "I think our conversation is over."

"Wait. I apologize. I was only reacting to the attitude I heard in your voice. Please accept my apology."

She rolled her eyes. "Apology accepted."

"Thank you. My reason for calling you 'impressive' is because each of the candidates that you endorsed won their race—even in Alabama. Didn't you feel special when the Speaker of the House invited you to address the House?"

"I didn't feel special. I felt needed."

The doors of the private elevator to the top floor opened. Hornsby gestured for her to enter. "Please." They entered. "I hear you have become good friends with the Speaker and other members of Congress on both sides of the aisle."

"Don't believe everything you hear."

"I don't." He grinned.

The elevator doors opened, and the plainclothes security guard, who looked like an Eastern European hit man, requested Yvonne's phone.

"Why?" she asked defiantly.

"It's a security procedure, Miss. I'll return it when you leave."

She removed the gold-chained navy-blue purse that hung over her shoulder, opened it, and handed him the locked phone.

"Any keys or coins in your purse?" he asked.

"No," she annoyingly said.

He scanned her purse and body with the wand.

"It's just a precaution," Hornsby said and led her into the presidential suite without a member of the security team. "Please have a seat."

Yvonne sat in the middle on the eight-person semicircular sofa.

Hornsby sat directly across on an oversized silk chair that matched the sofa. A mirrored glass coffee table separated them.

He leaned forward, fingers arched on thighs. "You look like a woman that doesn't tolerate bullshit, so let me be frank. I have a message for your son."

He seemed to expect her neutral expression to change. When it didn't, he said, "I'm sure he told you that we met."

Yvonne kept her straight womanly posture and mouth closed.

He seemed confused by her demeanor and leaned back. "Your son is too ambitious. He's greedy. He's trying to get into my pockets. But before he can get into my mine, he has to go through the pockets of those who count their dimes. They become very dangerous and uncontrollable when their dimes decrease."

She gave him a wry smile. "So, you're the one that my son outsmarted. You're the heartless bastard that killed children. What do you see when you look at yourself in the mirror?"

He leaned forward and looked into her eyes as if in search of her weakness. Then he leaned back, elbows on his thighs and hands clasped. "Your son didn't tell you? I see God because I am God. He should've told you the only reason that you and he are alive is that I have allowed it."

"Wrong! My son and I are alive because God has sealed us. You are not God. You are the wickedness in high places, the man of sin and son of perdition. You are the devil, Mr. Hornsby!"

"Then, you should fear me, because all power is in my hand."

Yvonne calmed herself. "Your power, Mr. Hornsby, is temporary. It's given from God to fulfill His purpose."

"His purpose? What is *my* purpose?"

She stared. "I know who you are, Mr. Hornsby. Your purpose is to oppose the things of God and exalt yourself."

"Why would your God send someone to oppose him if he is almighty? Is he bored?"

"He's not bored—just selective. Your purpose is to remove the unworthy. You exist to fulfill the Scripture, 'Evil shall slay the wicked...' (Psalm 34:21) You are like the one sitting in the temple of God, pretending to be God, spewing strong delusions that people might believe your lies."

"Like your son, you underestimate me."

Her eyes widened. "We don't underestimate you. We know the only power given to the devil comes from God for His purpose. You have no power over us. You fear us."

Hornsby rested his arms on his thighs. His hands were crossed in-between his legs. "Fear you? I don't fear you. You are nothing to fear. You're a smart woman, but still a woman. Your son is a smart nigger, but still a nigger."

Yvonne leaned forward, both hands flat on her lap. "You know what I see when I look in the mirror? I see Harriet Tubman and Rosa Parks, women I would've been if I was living during that time. You should fear the black woman."

"And why is that?"

She inched forward. "Because what the black man hasn't started, the black woman will. And what the black man doesn't finish, the black woman will."

His eyes narrowed.

She stood boldly; he stood as if to intimate her.

She ignored him and headed for the door without looking back.

With one hand on the doorknob, Yvonne turned to him. His derogatory thoughts for her were written on his face. "There are six things the Lord hates. You are all seven abominations."

She held direct eye contact for several seconds. When he didn't speak, she turned and left the suite.

The guard returned her cell, and she entered the elevator that sped back to the crowded lobby.

As she maneuvered to leave the hotel, she phoned Derrick, with video on.

"Ma, I'm overriding your decision not to have bodyguards."

"No, you're not! I told you, Jesus is my bodyguard. Nothing can happen to me until God allows it."

"C'mon, Ma. Wisdom overshadows love."

"Yes, it does. That's why Jesus walked in Galilee but not in Jewry, because the Jews sought to kill him. Like Jesus, I know where and where not to go, when and when not."

Derrick's expression projected his thoughts.

She read his eyes. "I know you disagree with my reasoning, but I'm not afraid to walk through the valley of death."

He lowered his head and slid his left hand down his face. "Ma, I can't lose you. That's why I didn't want you involved."

"You won't lose me, and I won't lose you. Faith, virtue, knowledge, temperance, patience, godliness, brotherly kindness, and charity—those things have abounded in us since our youth. And Scripture says, '...for if ye do these things, ye shall never fall.' (2 Peter 1:10)

"We will not fall because we are called and chosen. We know what his next moves are. He's not resigning as the secretary of state to be Donaldson's VP. He's planning to get rid of Donaldson."

"You mean, kill him?"

"He's not going to be VP for four years."

"Maybe he will force Donaldson to resign."

"Donaldson is too arrogant to resign. I can't even see him leaving the White House if he loses his reelection."

"You're right. He's positioning himself to be president for a reason. He might be the Antichrist."

"He's definitely one of them."

Derrick exhaled in the truth of those words. "Whatever happens, we got the underground ready."

* * *

Yvonne followed Quelle's strategy to speak directly to the voters in the red counties and appeared on XOF news. She was expecting to discuss politics, when the brash, long-necked, black female host said, "Isn't your son, Derrick Williams, financing terrorists?"

Yvonne calmly replied, "I didn't come on the show to talk about my son. But I'm glad you brought up his name. Those allegations have been proven false by the president's justice department. Your concern and the viewers' should be on persons who side with foreign governments over American intelligence. Think about it. When someone speaks against the men and women who sacrifice their lives to protect Americans from domestic and foreign terrorist attacks, isn't that person an enemy of the State?"

"Are you calling the president an enemy of the State?"

"He has already made that known by his actions. I am on your show to confirm it, that the viewers who don't watch the real news might hear it."

The host knitted her brows, with her long fake eyelashes tight and straight. Her narrowed head lowered slightly with tense and strained eyes. "We are the real news!"

"No, you're not, and it's about time that someone said it to your face. This station is fake news and Russian propaganda talking points."

"Let's go back to the real news. The Left is planning to impeach the president on trumped-up charges. Are you afraid that will guarantee the president's reelection?"

"I'm not."

"As one from the far left, you should be. The American people are against Congress overturning an election. That was proven when President Rodham was impeached for his heinous crime but was reelected. History is repeating itself, except that you and your party on the Left are planning to impeach a president who hasn't committed a crime." The host swatted her right hand into the air. "Go ahead with impeachment. America will see right through it and reelect the president—and the Left will lose control in both chambers of Congress."

"First, the Unity Corporation voting initiative isn't the far left or the Left. We are independents who support moral candidates regardless of party.

"Second, President Rodham had mutual sex. Adultery isn't a crime in this country. His crime was lying about it under oath. But he was contrite, and the people forgave him because who wouldn't lie to keep their wife and daughter from worldwide embarrassment.

"But President Donaldson... he openly abused power, committed bribery, obstructed Congress and justice, and lied religiously to the American people without apology."

"Those allegations are from the fake news outlets that you watch and believe. There has been no evidence presented other than hearsay that the president committed a crime. No president in history had an economy as great as this one. No president in history had unemployment as low as this one. President Donaldson has made America great again. And his reelection will keep America great. The American people are looking at the things that matter."

Yvonne gave a slight grin. "There is a difference between things that matter and matter most. Our jobs matter, our healthcare matters, the economy matters, unemployment matters. But what matters most is our democracy, our freedom from dictatorship.

"The framers of the Constitution set up three equal branches of government to guard against a monarchy and dictator. But this president has placed himself above the law and was not being held accountable by Congress. The American people agreed and voted for the Left to control Congress to keep the president in check, so why should they be concerned about losing seats when they were given those seats by the people to guard against tyranny.

"The concern you as a black person, and Jews, and Muslims, and nonwhite immigrants, should have is that America is on the path to becoming the resurrection of Nazi Germany. If that happens, I will be among the heads of the resistance."

The host abruptly ended the interview.

Yvonne's words led to increased claims that she and her son are terrorist sympathizers. Death threats mounted, but Yvonne continued to refuse bodyguards.

* * *

Family members and close friends were gathered at Derrick's home. A massive three-layer yellow cake with chocolate frosting baked by Grandma Ruth sat in front of him with candles "3" and "0" on it.

Juna lit the candles.

Charlene initiated the happy birthday song. Shareese and Blue were swaying with their hands up in the air, and the others followed.

Juna surprised everyone except Derrick with her stellar voice that scaled beyond what the others could reach. Xavier and Amari added bass harmony.

When the minute-long song ended, Juna said, "Okay, make a wish."

Derrick closed his eyes. *I wish for the Lord to continue protecting my wife and kids, and all my family and friends in spirit and soul.*

He opened his eyes and blew out the candles.

The hundred and eighteen guests applauded.

Jamaal, a self-taught artist, whose artwork Derrick had purchased for his home and commissioned at his stores, presented a wrapped portrait.

"What is this?" Derrick asked.

"Unwrap it," Jamaal said with the smiley face.

Derrick curiously tore the wrapping. "Wow! I love it!" He lifted the portrait for everyone to see.

Amidst the oohs and ahhs, Yvonne said, "That's very nice, Jamaal. Who is the woman beneath my son with her back to us?"

"Take a guess?"

"Looks like me from the back."

"It is you."

Charlene, sitting on Amari's lap, said, "Tell us what the portrait means?"

Jamaal pointed. "Everybody can see the backdrop is New York City. Derrick's face at the top represents the focused and wise young man who's watching his mother's back from his place at the head of the conglomerate."

Yvonne eagerly asked, "Why are there two pictures of me facing the mirrors? Is that a reflection?"

"It is a reflection. They look the same from the outside—but on the inside one is the civic-minded you—the other is the rebel you. Both are looking in the mirror to watch Derrick's back."

"That's one hundred," Stephanie said.

"For sure," Derrick said and immediately replaced one of the hung abstract paintings in the foyer with it.

* * *

When the party entered its second hour, Derrick and Quelle were chatting on the black linen sofa. The 2018 tune by Famous Dex had several on the improvised dance floor.

"Thanks again for inviting me. I was surprised when your mother told me that you wanted me to come."

"I'm glad you came. You are a very impressive young man."

"Thank you, Mr. Williams."

"Please call me, Derrick."

"Gotcha."

Derrick nodded, smiling. "What are your plans for the future?"

"I want to be a political strategist."

"Want to be? You already are. You're the reason why Alabama has an independent senator."

"Thank you, but I couldn't've done it without my team of volunteers."

"Volunteers rally around the cause they believe in. It takes leadership to keep them. You provided great leadership."

"Thank you."

"Are you going to stay with us during the presidential election?"

"Of course."

"Has my mother assigned you to a state? Alabama is a waste of your talent. The president will win Alabama."

"We know. Your mother assigned me to western Pennsylvania and Wisconsin."

"Be careful. The North has become more dangerous than the South for political activists on the Left."

"I will be."

Derrick patted him on the shoulder. "Do you have a girlfriend?"

"I'm gay."

"Oh. Does my mother know?"

"She knows. How do you feel about me being gay?"

"Jesus said, 'Judge not according to the appearance, but judge righteous judgment.' (St. John 7:24) I define righteous judgment as written in Jeremiah 17:10—'I, the Lord, search the heart, I try the reins, even to give every man according to his ways, and according to the fruit of his doings.' God will judge every person by the righteousness in their heart, not by their sexual preference, or race, or religion.'"

"I agree," Quelle replied.

Derrick placed his arm around him. "Do you play spades?"

"Yeah."

"Good. Wanna be my partner?"

"Sure."

"I'll get the cards."

* * *

In the third hour, the ambiance and electronic tunes by Darius had the guests dancing and lounging as if they were inside a nightclub. Juna, Charlene, and Judy were at the kitchen table in girl talk. Yvonne, Gladys, and Xavier were in the solarium.

Derrick and Michael were chatting at the dining table.

"How are things holding with you and Judy?"

"We good. How are things going with you?"

"I'm not concerned about me. My concern is my family. My mother has made herself a target and refuses to accept bodyguards. But she knows I got someone watching over her 24/7. Charlene isn't a threat to my enemies, so her safety is not on the line. My biggest concern is leaving Juna and the children when I'm on travel."

"Take them with you."

"Sometimes I can't. Besides, she's safer when I'm not around. But in case she has to defend herself, I took her to the range a few times. Her first shot struck the target in the forehead."

"Whoa. Was that beginner's luck?"

"Nah. She did it six times in fourteen shots. She's a natural. My mother doesn't know this, but I got guns hidden on both floors. I'm ready if they try to bust up in here."

"I keep a gun with me too. I was called a nigga lover by one of Judy's in-laws at the dinner table when I went to her parents' for Thanksgiving. He said if I weren't with Judy, I would be dead. Judy's parents and others at the table scolded him and apologized, saying he was drunk. But I know drunkenness brings out true feelings."

"It does. It also gives nerve to the coward."

Michael nodded.

"Be ready to move in a minute's notice," Derrick said.

"Why?"

"Because Erich Hornsby is the one trying to bring me down. He's the brains behind Donaldson. So why is he the VP?

I believe he's planning to get rid of Donaldson so he can overthrow the government."

"With the impeachment?"

"Maybe. But this I know: Hornsby will come after me and all who are close to me. Things will move faster if Donaldson is convicted in the Senate or loses the election, but the direction won't change if he wins. If the Senate convicts him, which I doubt because it takes two-thirds of the Senate to convict, be ready to leave the country. If he wins or loses the election, be on a plane the next morning."

"What about my family and Judy?"

"Take them with you if you trust them. If not, don't tell them where you're going."

"How long do I need to stay away?"

"If Donaldson loses, wait until after the inauguration. If he wins, be prepared to wait a few years. Make sure you take enough money to stay afloat. If you need help with moving your money, let me know, and I will have Mustafa contact you. But wherever you go, stay incognito."

"Derrick, I can see the danger in your eyes and feel it in your voice."

"It's about to go down, Michael. What many feared, and some believed couldn't happen in this country, is about to happen, and it's not a movie. So, until election night, party like its 1999."

They smiled. Michael gestured to the music and said, "Who's this?"

"Dennis Buné. I heard it when Juna and I were at the club in South Beach."

Moments later, they turned their attention to the makeshift dance floor, and the tune by Roland Tings had everyone dancing up close. Judy was gesturing with her fingers for Michael to join her on the dance floor, and he did.

Juna darted over to Derrick and led him by the hand to join the others that were moved by the 2017 beat by Tinlicker & Helsloot.

Juna was dancing the *Dip* in her long loose-fitted dark-blue printed dress. Derrick was dancing the *Double Dab* in his loose-fitted blue jeans and Lebron James jersey. When the song ended with the beat of another, both were dancing the *Woah*—then Derrick turned to the *Shoulder Shake*—and Juna was *Swaggin.*

Everyone on the dance floor stopped to watch the contest. Shareese led the cheers for Juna. Blue led the cheers for Derrick. The contest ended when Derrick danced the *Shoot.*

CHAPTER 9

The next evening, Juna lay on the bed, speaking Tagalog to Malachi. Rhea-Toni was downstairs in Emy's room. Derrick was sitting on the bedroom's sofa reading *Hidden Behind Their Smiles* by Cassandra Dyer.

The home phone rang, and the robotic voice came from the overhead speakers, *"Caller Doctor Bash."*

"Answer," Derrick said.

"Williams residence."

"Hello, is Mrs. Williams there?"

"Hi, Doctor Bash."

"Hi, Juna. I'm sorry to be calling so late, but I was looking over your x-ray. I need to speak with you and your husband."

"He's here."

"Hi, Doctor Bash."

"Hello, Derrick. Can you and Juna come to my office tonight?"

"Tonight? It's after eight. Can it wait until the morning?"

"I prefer not. It's very important."

Walking toward Juna, Derrick said, "You can't tell us now?"

"I need to show you what concerns me."

Juna screeched, "What's wrong?"

"Don't get upset. I only need to show you something."

Derrick sat next to Juna and placed his arm around her. "Okay, Dr. Bash. We'll be there."

"Thanks. You can park in my spot at the back. Press the buzzer, and I will remotely open the door."

"Okay."

Derrick and Juna quickly led Malachi downstairs to Emy's room.

Juna had tears running down her face.

"What wrong?" Emy asked.

"The doctor called with a concern," Derrick said. "He needs to see us tonight."

Emy's expression of worry increased.

"It's okay. I'm sure it's only something minor," Derrick said.

With his arm wrapped around Juna as she lay against his chest, crying, they rode the elevator to the garage and entered the $200,000 car that Derrick had purchased for Juna's birthday. While he drove, Juna was tearfully speculating.

"It's something minor. Don't worry," he repeated.

The eight-mile drive ended when Derrick pulled into the well-lit parking area at the back of the single-level building. Juna, anxious, exited the vehicle before the engine was shut off and waited in front of the car. Derrick wrapped his arm around her shoulders as they walked to the back entrance.

Derrick pressed the buzzer, and the door immediately unlocked. They entered as Juna wiped her last tear.

Doctor Bash was standing at the end of the brightly lit carpeted narrow hallway with both hands inside the pockets of the white lab coat. He had a pleasant smile that seemingly eased Juna's nervousness.

"Thank you for coming," he said and led them into his office.

The two sat in front of the blank monitor on the doctor's unusually cluttered desk. Derrick wrapped his arm around a trembling Juna.

Dr. Bash stood next to the monitor. "This is what I want to show you." He turned on the screen and pointed at the x-ray. "The child appears to be malformed."

"What's that?" Juna asked.

Derrick's eyes shifted to Dr. Bash. "Deformed? How is that possible? The x-rays last month didn't show any deformity."

Juna was weeping when she heard the word "deformed."

"I'm sorry, Mr. Williams, but malformation can occur late in pregnancy."

"After seven months?"

"Yes. This x-ray was taken last week when your wife was here for her monthly visit. I was out of the office. I'm just looking at it now. I apologize for the delay."

Derrick instinctively took a picture of the screen with his cell phone, then lowered his head and shook it. He turned his attention to a whimpering Juna and hugged her. "It's okay. We will love him the same."

His eyes lifted to Dr. Bash. "We have to go. Thank you for informing us."

"I'm sorry," Dr. Bash said.

Derrick wrapped his arms around her, and they exited the way they had entered. Her cries continued as they stepped out into the surprising darkness.

Derrick halted. "What happened to the lights?"

Juna's sobbing was the only clear sound as he scanned his surroundings in the moonlight. The thought to reenter the building crossed his mind, but he stood in place and remotely unlocked the car doors while he continued to scan the area.

He led Juna to the car with his left arm wrapped tightly around her shoulders and opened the passenger's door.

Juna entered the car with increased tears.

Derrick closed the door with his eyes on the darkness that covered the trees twenty yards away.

He slowly walked around to the driver's door with his eyes on the trees behind the car and waited a few seconds. He didn't see anything. *I'm paranoid.* He opened the driver's door and entered.

His attention immediately went to Juna, who had puffy and bloodshot eyes. He kissed her gently. "Everything will be okay."

Derrick started the engine and nonchalantly shifted the gear to reverse. In the rearview camera, he saw a person approaching with a silver handgun pointed at the car.

Thoughts raced through his mind. He couldn't go forward because of the building. If he sped back, the gunman might shoot and hit Juna. With his eyes locked on the fast-approaching figure, he held Juna's hand. She was unaware of the present danger.

"Get out of the car!" the gunman yelled with the gun pointed at the driver's window.

Juna screamed hysterically.

Unruffled, Derrick faced her. "Stay calm. We'll be okay."

Her breathing was ragged.

With his foot on the brake, Derrick lowered the window. "I'm not getting out."

Derrick caught the face of a teen inside the black, hooded pullover. His heartless expression changed when he saw Derrick's face up close. He sensed that the teen recognized him. "You know who I am?"

With the back of his unarmed hand, the teen wiped the sweat from his forehead.

"You never shot a person before, have you?" Derrick said.

"Man, get out of the car," a cracking voice replied.

"If I get out, I will make it easy for you. If you shoot me, you will have to shoot my pregnant wife. Are you ready to kill three people for a few dollars?"

"She wasn't supposed to be here."

"But she is. I wasn't supposed to be here, but I am. The person who sent you knew my wife would be here. He didn't tell you? Why?"

"Get out of the car!"

Derrick stayed calm. "You were supposed to shoot us before we got into the car. It was supposed to look like a carjacking. If you shoot us now, it will look like an assassination."

The teen didn't say a word. His eyes reflected the confusion in his thoughts.

Derrick seized on the moment. "I can offer you something that you don't have."

"What's that?"

"A future."

"A future?"

"Yes. Redemption."

"Man, I don't need redemption. I need money. I got to do this, or I won't have a future."

"Do you really think you will have a future if you kill me? You're not a member of a gang. You're nothing but a two-bit car thief, and that's why you were sent. How much did they give you to kill me? A thousand dollars?"

His expression turned.

"Oh, they gave you less? The white man gave someone a million dollars to kill me. That person probably paid the one who sent you a hundred thousand. You are getting less than a thousand to kill three people. You were told to shoot me before I got into the car and to take the car to the chop shop where you would get another thousand or two for the vehicle."

Perplexed, the teen asked, "How do you know that?"

"Because if you were an assassin, you wouldn't've asked me to get out of the car. You would've shot through the window. You were sent to shoot us but to make it look like a carjacking. I'm sure you have a record for stealing cars. That's why you were chosen. It's common sense. That is something you don't use."

"Muthafucka, imma blow your head off!"

"Go ahead. Yours will be blown off before sunrise."

"What the fuck you talkin' 'bout?"

"Let me tell you what would've happened if you had shot us before we entered the car. You would've taken the vehicle to the chop shop, expecting to get paid for the car. There, you and whoever was working, would've been killed. The morning news would've said that Derrick Williams and his pregnant wife were murdered by a car thief who was killed at the chop shop. It appears that gang members who support Derrick Williams discovered the whereabouts of his killer and took revenge for this black-on-black crime. That was the white man's plan, but God intervened. You hesitated because there is some good in your heart. If it wasn't, you wouldn't've cared that my wife is pregnant and would've shot us before we got into the car. God has saved you and us."

The teen paused, seemingly in search of words to say from his jumbled thoughts.

Derrick pointed. "You see that camera at the edge of the building? It has night vision."

He turned and looked.

"Don't run."

The teen swung his head back to Derrick with panic written on his face.

"If you run, I can't help you."

"How can you help me?"

"I offered you a future. The offer is still on the table."

"I'm listening."

"Who sent you?"

"The head of one-eighty-seven."

"Reginald West came out of that hood."

"Word. He sponsors a summer league in the Bronx and gives the proceeds to one-eighty-seven."

"I need you to tell the police who sent you."

"Snitch! I ain't no snitch."

"Telling the truth isn't snitching. It's being honest."

"Fuck that. You trying to get me killed."

"You're already dead. I'm trying to bring you back to life."

"Fuck this." He lowered his head and shook it. "I'm out."

"If you run away, I will call the police. You're on videotape. Do you think you will see the sunrise? One-eighty-seven is going to kill you before the police catch you."

He lowered the gun. "Man, the only future you're offering is behind bars. Snitches get killed in prison."

"I'm not offering prison. I have a very good lawyer who will bail you out within minutes after your arrest. You won't have to do any time if you tell the truth."

"Why can't you just do that without me having to snitch?"

"Because the offer includes redemption, which you cannot get without confession."

"You a preacher or something?"

"Every wise man is a minister, so I'm speaking the words that God put in my mouth for you to hear. You came here to kill a man for a few dollars. What if someone shot your mother for a few dollars? You need to think about that."

His eyes glared as if he visualized someone shooting his mother for the amount he had received.

Derrick sensed his thoughts. "Now you know what the son, or daughter, or wife of the man that you were sent to kill would've felt. How old are you?"

Without looking Derrick in the eye, he said, "Sixteen."

"What's your name?"

"Calvin."

"Calvin, do you believe in God?"

"Yeah."

"Then you know that God is looking at you right now, and He is pleased."

"Pleased? Why? I was gonna kill you."

"But you didn't. Tell me why you didn't?"

"I don't know."

"You always know why you did or didn't do something. Tell me why you didn't kill me?"

"Uh, 'cause I saw you on television. You look out for black people."

"You respect me?"

"Yeah."

"Then why are you robbing and ready to kill black people?"

"M-man, I don't know."

"You know. To be healed. You need to say it."

"Man, I don't know! I guess I'm fucked up!"

"That's what happens when you become a slave to wickedness."

"You saying I'm the devil?"

"You're not the devil. You're not evil."

"You just said I was wicked. What's the difference?"

"Wicked people do bad things out of ignorance and stupidity. Evil people do bad things from the heart. Wicked people think that evil people are on their side, but they're not. Evil was ready to slay you if you had done its will."

Calvin wrinkled his forehead. The sound of the gun falling onto the pavement broke silence. He turned and squatted on the ground with his back against the driver's door and sobbed, head down.

Derrick shifted the car into park and embraced Juna, who was trembling. "Are you okay?"

Her voice cracked, "Let's go! I want to go!"

"Not yet. I have to call the police."

"Call them when we leave!" she said angrily.

"I have to be here when the police come."

"Maybe Doctor Bash still here. I go inside with him."

"No! He's a part of this. Calm down. It's over."

Derrick voice-activated the car to phone 911. Then he phoned his lawyer.

"What's up, Derrick?" Mustafa said.

"They just tried to kill my wife and me."

"Y'all alright?"

"We are. We're waiting for the police."

"What happened?"

"They tried to make it look like a carjacking, but I was able to talk him out of it."

"Where is he?"

"He surrendered to me. I need you to bail him out and take him to one of the condos. He can't go back to his neighborhood. Let him call his mother from an encrypted line. I want you to relocate his family."

"Why are you so generous to the hoodlum that came to kill you?"

"I'll explain later. I hear the sirens."

Flashing red and blue lights from several approaching squad cars entered the parking lot. They turned on their searchlights.

The officers leaped out of their vehicles with guns pointed at the teen, who immediately raised his hands and shouted, "Hands up! Don't shoot!"

They confiscated the gun and yanked him to his feet, cuffed him on the hood of the police car, and sat him in the back of one of the caged vehicles.

The lead officer approached. "Mr. Williams, is everyone okay?"

"We are."

"What happened?"

"He was sent to kill me, but changed his mind and is willing to talk. I believe the doctor in that building was a part of it."

"What makes you believe that?"

"The teen knew we would be here. The doctor called and said it was an emergency for us to come. When we got here, the parking lot lights were on. When we left the building, it was like this. He told us that our child is deformed. I took a picture of the x-ray. I believe he set us up."

"I'll send an officer over to take your statement. You and your wife are very lucky."

"Luck didn't have nothing to do with this. God saved our lives tonight."

* * *

Music by Quality Control was cranking from the six-nine that sat at the side of the dark entrance into the cul-de-sac that led to the chop shop.

"Where that muthafucka at?" the lone person in the vehicle said.

After he had waited two more minutes, he dialed.

"Bags, your boy hasn't shown up."

Where that nigga at? "Something ain't right. Maybe the doctor kept them longer than he should've."

"Or that muthafucka punked out. I told I should've done it."

"And I told you that we have to keep our hands clean on this one. He'll be there."

"He's fifteen minutes late. The shop is about to close."

"Damn! Fuck it. Take his ass out. But make sure you kill him inside the car."

"Ah-right."

Bags lit another blunt. After a few puffs, his cell rang again. "Yeah."

"What up, nigga? I'm watching the news and I ain't seen nothing."

"The doctor probably kept him and his wife longer than expected."

"I'm feeling something else. That nigga you sent reliable?"

"You told me that we had to keep our hands clean, so I sent a wannabe. He'll do it—he's a hungry nigga."

"I'll call you back in five minutes. You better have heard something by then."

Reginald West hung up the phone and nervously paced the white marble floor of his Miami glass home.

Bags phoned the gun that was waiting outside the chop shop. "The nigga showed yet?"

"Nah."

"Fuck. Did you make sure he was high?"

"He was high."

"I got another call. I'll call you back... Yeah, Reginald, what's up?"

"Your ass, muthafucka. The shit is on the news. That nigga you sent didn't shoot the muthafucka. He got arrested."

"Whaaat?"

"How could you fuck this up? My ass is in a bind."

"No problem. He won't talk. If he do, he won't make it to trial. I got people in the joint."

"Nigga, I trusted you to handle this shit, and you fucked it up."

"I'll take care of it."

"Wait, I gotta take this call."

Reginald clicked on call-waiting. The female computer voice said, "Mr. West, the item I purchased hasn't arrived. I am canceling the order and expect to be reimbursed for my transportation expenses as well."

The line went dead. *Shit.* In a haze, Reginald clicked to the previous line and unconsciously said out loud, "Because of Bags, I gotta give back the two million plus interest."

"Two million! Motherfucka, you told me that you got a hundred thousand."

"Uhh... I gave you fifty, nigga, and you didn't earn it."

"Fifty? Fuck that. Take your fifty back."

"Nah, nigga, I need you to finish the job, and I need it done by tomorrow night."

"Shiiit—not for fifty. I want seven figures."

"Seven figures? I ain't giving you half. Fuck you."

"Fuck you, do the shit yourself."

Reginald thought for a moment. "Alright, I'll give you a hundred."

"Five hundred."

"Five hundred? I can get somebody to do it for less than that."

"Then get that person."

"Alright, nigga, five hundred, but not until the job is done."

"Nah, nigga, in advance."

"What? You don't trust me?"

"Muthafucka, why should I trust you, you greedy bastard?"

"I'm in Miami, nigga. I leave for LA in the morning to start working on an album. I'll overnight a check."

"A check? Nigga, you crazy. The cracker that gave two mil didn't write a check. You got cash somewhere."

"Nigga, I won't be back for a week."

"Shit won't get done till you come back then. How important is this shit to you? You know someone who can bring cash."

"I ain't got five hundred laying around."

"Nigga, you got a house across the bridge. I know you got some cash in the safe."

"Yeah, but I ain't got five hundred."

"How much you got?"

"Two hundred."

"Alright, nigga. Give me that, and rest when you get back."

"I'll have it dropped off in the morning. I need Williams dead no later than tomorrow night. Make it look like a robbery."

"Done. I got a young gun locked and loaded. He won't hesitate to kill him, his wife, and his children. You feel me?"

"Word up from the college dropout. Bury the wife and kids with him."

CHAPTER 10

Bags, the Biz Markie look-alike, was arrested before the crack of dawn.

Before noon, the police arrested Dr. Bash and charged him with conspiracy to attempt murder when they discovered the x-ray was that of another woman.

When Reginald West didn't arrive in Los Angeles, the search discovered him murdered in his Miami home from an apparent robbery.

Derrick and Juna hadn't slept. The scenes from the night before replayed in their minds as an endless loop. They shared the experience with their families and close friends.

In the late afternoon, they were sitting on their bedroom sofa. Malachi and Rhea-Toni were downstairs with Emy. Derrick gently squeezed Juna's upper arms. "You have to stay strong."

"I'm strong. Just scared. It's scary, Derrick."

"I know it is. But you have a strong spirit. If you didn't, you would've left when I gave you the opening."

"What you mean? What opening?"

"When I said you could go back to Hawaii. But you didn't because your spirit is strong. Now I need your flesh to show the strength of your spirit. Don't show fear when you feel it."

"What you mean?"

"When I saw him running toward us with the gun pointed, I felt fear, but I knew I couldn't panic. I couldn't go forward because of the building. If I had pressed the gas with the car in reverse, what do you think he would've done?"

When she didn't answer, he said, "Out of panic he would've fired until he was out of bullets. I had to make a quick decision. I didn't make it; the spirit made it for me. As it turned out, it was the right decision.

"I didn't convince that teen not to shoot us. I only spoke the words that the Holy Ghost put in my mouth. If we listen, the Bible teaches us everything. Jesus said, 'And when they bring you unto the synagogues, and unto magistrates, and powers, take ye no thought how or what thing ye shall answer, or what ye shall say; For the Holy Ghost shall teach you in the same hour what ye ought to say.' (St. Luke 12:11-12)

"Another Scripture that is often recited but not understood, 'Trust in the Lord with all thine heart; and lean not unto thine own understanding. In all thy ways acknowledge him, and he shall direct thy paths.'" (Proverbs 3:5-6)

Juna was calm, as if the words had healed her. The side of her face lay on Derrick's chest, with her arms around him. "That why you confident he not shoot us?" she whispered.

"I felt something was wrong when the lights were out. My instincts told me that someone was hiding in those trees, but I didn't listen. I thought it was paranoia. That's why I didn't go for the gun that's strapped under the seat."

Juna's head jerked. "You have a gun in the car?"

"Yes."

"Why you not tell me before?"

"I'm sorry. I should've."

She cried.

He pulled her into his embrace. "I promise I will never keep another secret from you."

She nodded with her face sunk into his chest.

He gripped her arms, leaned back, and peered into her eyes. "As I had promised, I was ready to die with you. That's why I held your hand when I saw him running toward the car. I felt like it was too risky to try and get the gun. I accepted death. But when he said, 'get out the car,' I knew he wasn't an assassin. That's why I was calm and told you to be calm. When I lowered the window, I saw that he recognized me and didn't know I was the target. I could feel his thoughts.'"

"How did you know what he was told to do?"

"You mean about the chop shop?"

"Ooo, yes."

"What other reason would he have to tell us to get out of the car? It's not the type of car that you steal at gunpoint to commit a crime or take for a joy ride. I analyzed the situation at that moment. That's how the spirit works. I will always protect you before me. Trust the things I do and say."

The long and passionate kiss that Juna initiated was interrupted by the knock on their bedroom door.

"Come in," Derrick said.

Yvonne entered with her solemn expression.

Juna leaped from the sofa—"Mother Yvonne!"—and darted into her embrace. "God saves us," she said with teary eyes.

"Yes, He did," Yvonne said as she tightened the hug.

Derrick stood with his hands at the side.

With teary eyes, Yvonne looked over Juna's head against her breast and stared at her son, transmitting their thoughts to each other.

A few seconds passed, and Yvonne kissed the top of Juna's head. "Can we speak privately?" she said to Derrick.

Juna raised her head.

"Sure. Let's go into the library," Derrick said.

Juna straightened, and Yvonne said to her, "Our private conversation has nothing to do with you. I just need to speak with your husband. I have something to tell him about me that I don't want anyone to know about right now."

"I understand, Mother Yvonne."

Yvonne gently squeezed Juna's shoulders and followed Derrick into the library.

They sat next to each other on the black linen sofa and faced one another.

"I know about the gun you had under the driver's seat."

Surprised, he said, "How did you know about that?"

"Charlene told me. You know she tells me everything."

Derrick looked away to hide his frown.

"Don't be mad at her."

He turned back to his mother. "I told her not to tell you."

"First, there shouldn't be any secrets between us."

"I only had one secret because I know how you feel about guns."

"How do I feel about guns?"

"You don't like guns."

"I like guns. It's just that I know we will not win this war with guns. I'm happy you decided not to use your gun. You trusted in God, and He showed you why you should always put your trust in Him."

Angry, he said, "They knew my wife was pregnant and that she was with me. They sent a young gun to kill me, my wife, and my unborn child. I'm shooting next time."

"Why didn't you shoot this time?"

"Because I followed my instincts."

"Continue following your instincts. Don't say what you will or will not do the next time. Let your instincts and wisdom guide you when the moment occurs. It's the Holy Ghost."

"True. But I need to be ready. From now on, I'm going to keep a gun on me every time I leave the house. I know you think it's showing the lack of faith, but Jesus said, '...and he that hath no sword, let him sell his garment, and buy one.' (St. Luke 22:36) Peter was strapped with a sword when Jesus was captured. (St. John 18:10). A sword in those days was a gun."

"I have a gun," Yvonne said softly.

"What? When did you buy a gun?"

"Your father bought a gun for me because of the neighborhood. He took me to the range a couple of times."

"Where is the gun?"

"It's at my house. I don't carry it with me when I'm outside my house. I have it to protect myself when I'm in the house. Your father told me that God protects us when we leave our house, but the gun protects us inside the house."

"I thought to own a gun was against your religion. You were always preaching to us to stay away from guns. You wouldn't even buy us a toy gun."

"Because a toy gun will make you want to hold a real gun, and a real gun should only be in the hand of a responsible adult."

"Ma, you had a gun all this time? I can't believe it. So why are you refusing bodyguards?"

"Because God protects me from evil when I'm in the street. But if evil breaks into my house, my sword is ready."

Derrick felt uplifted and embraced her.

"I love you," Yvonne said in his ear. "And I will always protect you and your family. I got your back."

"And I got yours. I want you to live with me."

Yvonne lowered her head.

"Ma, I know you don't want to leave your house, but I need you here. I need you to protect my family."

"When Junior asked me to move in with him, I didn't, and he was killed." She tilted her head to the side and smiled. "I will move in."

They embraced.

* * *

Given her generous nature, Yvonne went to the homeless shelter and selected a family to own her North Carolina home. The only furniture she removed was Mister's bedroom. She placed those memorabilia in storage.

In the days that followed, Yvonne and Emy became very close. Both were happy to be around their grandchildren and often talked about God.

In the marriage that exceeded the happiness she had dreamed of, Juna gave birth to her third child, a boy named Anthony. Unlike Malachi and Rhea-Toni, Anthony had monolid eyes.

"Are we working on a fourth child?" Yvonne asked.

Juna giggled. "No, Mother Yvonne. I go back to accountant at Third Eye Films."

Startled, Yvonne said, "Derrick is letting you go into the office without him?"

"No, Mother Yvonne. I work from home. Everything I need on computer. I can Skype meetings."

"Oh. Good. How do you like the nannies that I hired?"

"Ooo, they good, Mother Yvonne. Big help."

"If you sense something is wrong or feel uncomfortable around one, please tell me immediately. I won't be offended. We are living in a world where we cannot take any chances."

"I know. The secret cameras help a lot. I see them with my children. They treated good."

"Happy to hear that."

Emy interjected, "Yeah, they good. Where you find them?"

"One is a high school graduate, and the other majored in childcare."

Emy said, "I know—I talk to them—but how you find them?"

"Derrick is part owner of a childcare provider in Brooklyn. I got the résumés from the center and interviewed them. I selected the top four and ran a check on their criminal history, the sex offender registry, child abuse records, and driving records. Then I checked their references."

"Wow… you're good."

"Thanks. But keep an eye out because anyone can have a bad day."

"We will."

* * *

Derrick was in Baltimore to survey the properties the Unity Corporation had purchased for the neighborhood economic development. During the two-day visit, he noticed the cleaners across the street from his 24/7 superstore project.

He pointed. "Who owns that cleaners?"

The mayor said, "Koreans."

"Are they supportive of the community?"

"In what way?" the mayor asked.

The neighborhood representative who was with the group of six interjected, "No. We tried to get them to sponsor basketball uniforms, kids for summer camp, holiday parties, but not a dime."

The mayor said, "Well, I'm sure they will be more open to sponsorship now that they know the Unity Corporation superstore is coming to the neighborhood."

Derrick stared at the cleaners as black customers were entering and exiting.

After a few seconds, he said, "That's not acceptable. We have a Korean cleaner in our Washington, DC, community who was supportive before we arrived."

He turned and looked at the space purchased for his superstore. After analyzing the property, he pointed. "We can allocate a portion of the parking lot and shorten the store to accommodate our cleaners."

"You will put the cleaner across the street out of business," the mayor distressfully said.

Derrick's eyes connected without a response. He shifted to the neighborhood representative, and she was smiling.

Derrick shifted back to the group. "I want to thank you for giving me a tour of the neighborhood. Construction will begin next month." He shook their hands and departed with his two bodyguards.

As he rode in the back seat of the rented SUV, he phoned Juna.

"My love!" she enthusiastically said.

"Yes, my love. Let me see Anthony."

Juna lifted Anthony to face the portal.

"I love you, Anthony." Derrick kissed the screen. "Is everything good there?"

"Yes."

"Where is your mother?"

"Downstairs with Malachi."

"My mother's there?"

"She working downstairs."

"Where's Rhea-Toni?"

"She with the nanny. I watch her."

"Let's go out tonight."

"Where?" Juna said with excitement.

"Wherever you want?"

"Club."

"Reggae, House, or Hip-Hop?"

"All three."

"All three it is."

After the call, he phoned his mother. "We need a challenger to the mayor in Baltimore. He's all about lining his own pockets."

"On it," she said.

CHAPTER 11

Inside the building across from the White House, Hornsby was on an encrypted video call with the council members. "We are running out of time."

"Let's initiate the plan," Murt said.

Hornsby's somber expression didn't change. "That's a risk not worth taking. Another issue is Kabir. He went into hiding as if tipped off. We have to find him to kill him."

"Williams has significantly increased his popularity in the black communities. His assassination will cause riots," the General said.

"Maybe. But I doubt it will cause the riots we need to declare martial law. Williams isn't Martin Luther King-like. He doesn't go to church."

"He does now," Jake said. "He's attending that church of fools who think they are the true Jews."

That information brought concern to Hornsby. "Is that the church of prophet William that praises Jesus?"

"Yes."

"Now we have another conundrum. If niggers start believing en masse that they are the true Jews, they will wake the force we cannot defeat."

"What force is that?" Jake asked.

"The truth."

"The truth? Niggers are the aboriginal Jews?"

"They are. That's the one thing Hitler didn't know. Is Williams one of their preachers?"

"No. But he's making a movie called *The Maccabees* and another called *The Lost Tribe of Judah*."

"*Adam and Eve* wasn't a one-off," Hornsby said. "He's preaching in movies. If niggers become influenced by those movies, we will have another serious threat. But we have to deal with that later. This call is about our next steps. The Senate impeachment trial begins next week. We have to continue stonewalling the witnesses and documents. If we don't, Donaldson will be convicted."

"But won't that help us? You will become president," Jake said.

Hornsby gritted his teeth. *You are dumber than Arthur.* "If the documents are released, I will also be impeached and convicted, along with some of our allies in Congress."

"We still have another fifteen months before the election," Stephen said. "How can we stonewall that long?"

Hornsby answered, "To our benefit, this administration has appointed over two hundred federal judges, and we control the Supreme Court. We can claim executive privilege and keep the witnesses and documents tied up in the courts with appeals."

"You think that we will work with the Left in control of the Senate?" Stephen asked.

Hornsby replied, "The Left is eager to convict Donaldson. They don't want to wait on the courts. They believe they have enough evidence at hand, and they do, but not enough to convince sixteen senators from our party to convict. If we can bribe enough of the moderates in our party to ignore the evidence, and keep Donaldson scripted, we can win reelection by boasting the strongest economy in history, the lowest unemployment in history, the record-high stock market, the defeat of ISIS, and the need for restoring Hadrian's wall. The moderates in our party are tired of Donaldson, but with me on the ticket, we can gain their support because they see me as the adult in the room."

"He's too undisciplined to stay on script," the General said. "Why not eliminate him, and you run as the head of the ticket?"

"I have become very popular among the base, but not yet as popular as him," Hornsby said. "So we need to use him to energize the base. We can quickly remove him after the election."

"You know that fool won't stay on script."

"I know. But we have learned that fools like following one who doesn't appear to be a fool. There's a reason why we recognize All Fools Day, April 1. There are enough of them to help us reelect Donaldson."

"Why don't we just let the Senate convict him on the evidence sent from the House?"

Hornsby replied, "That might entice his followers to start the civil war without us. We have to ensure that he is not convicted."

"More damning evidence is coming out every day," the General said. "I don't think we can keep enough of the moderates from crossing over. Several are retiring and some are up for reelection in purple states. They might wilt under the pressure."

Hornsby barked, "The ones retiring aren't going home to sit on the couch with the remote! They got a seven-figure salary waiting for them. They won't buck if they know we will take that job away—and we will if they turn on us. They remember what happened to Senator Polo in Florida. He was planning to retire until we took away the job. Now he's one of our lackeys like the two in South Carolina. Donaldson will be acquitted if we continue to stonewall."

* * *

The political climate had already divided the country, but the impeachment trial widened the division. Tribalism revealed the racism that many in Congress claimed they didn't have. White Supremacists were marching without hoods, holding torches in the night, shouting, "Jews will not replace us!" White men in American-made pickup trucks were at the ready with their long guns. Some became impatient and attacked synagogues, and areas frequented by nonwhite immigrants and blacks.

Derrick took advantage of the Leadership Council's preoccupation with the impeachment hearings and trial to expand his exports and bank business in the worldwide market. The Unity Corporation farmers struck a deal that made them the leading exporters of various fruits, vegetables, nuts, crops, dairy products, and meats to countries around the world.

Unity Corporation's agricultural products and ready-to-eat foods included their chain of fast-food businesses in West and South Africa. The bank had major transformational projects in Africa, Asia, and South America.

Their investors, which included the credit union shareholders and the underground stock market, added to their millions or to those who made their first million.

Derrick had climbed the ladder of billionaires, and generational wealth in the black communities was growing exponentially.

* * *

Hornsby was livid at the council members. "I told you when I saw that nigger in Davos to block him from expanding into the worldwide markets. How could you let that nigger export?"

"Sir, we were focused on the impeachment," Jake said.

"Didn't I tell you that I am handling the impeachment? Murt's handling the reelection campaign, the General is our eyes and ears in the Pentagon, and the rest of you were supposed to keep an eye on our money."

"The nigger has a lot of subsidiaries, and some are white faces," Jake said. "We didn't know."

Hornsby shifted his frown to Stephen. "How did you let that nigger open a bank into the worldwide markets?"

"He did what we do—hid behind the credit union."

"We can't wait any longer. My profits are down to eleven million dollars a day. In two weeks, I've lost eighty-four million dollars in profits because of that nigger. Take him out! I want him dead before the sunrise."

"We can't," Murt said. "It's too risky. That might scare the moderates. I suggest we ride it out until after the election. We can't stop any of the deals he has already made, but we can block any new deals."

Hornsby nodded with reddish eyes looking through his lowered brows. "The day after the election, I want Williams and his mother, dead!"

* * *

In the battleground of Michigan, Yvonne was speaking to a crowd that exceeded fifteen thousand voters comprised of undecided Democrats, Republicans, and Independents. A huge banner that read, "Country Before Party," hung clearly behind her. On the front of the podium was the fitted sign that read the same.

"I'm here today in the hope that I might convince you on who should not be president. Let's start with this question. What is the duty of the president?

"First and foremost is honesty. Second is protecting the citizens. If the president lies an average of ten times a day, he is not protecting the citizens. Campaign promises are the reason we vote for a candidate.

"Like many of you, I'm tired of hearing candidates on both sides of the aisle talking about what they are going to do for the middle class. I'm tired of hearing them claim that they care about the middle class. I'm tired of hearing the promises they conveniently forget when they are elected.

"There are some who see the middle class as households that earn over $400,000 a year. Where I come from, that is not the middle class. So, when politicians say they are for the middle class, ask which middle class? The elite middle class, or the working people middle class? I'm standing for the working people middle class, the households that earn between $100,000 and $200,000 a year. How can we get more Americans into that middle class?

"Forget what you heard. This country caters to classes. The lower, the middle-lower, the upper-lower, the lower-middle, the middle, the upper-middle, lower-upper, the middle-upper, and the upper that is the one percent who controls the wealth in this country.

"I came from the lower, and by the grace of God, my children were able to remove me from generational welfare. So, what do I owe for God's grace? I owe the same love that He showed for me, that I might help others free themselves from the clutches of poverty. My fight is against greed and selfishness because those give birth to corruption.

"I am a registered Democrat. But that doesn't mean I won't vote for a Republican or an Independent. I am a registered Democrat. But that doesn't mean I will continue to support a Democrat if his or her actions are corrupt. I will not! I believe in country before the party!

"I was asked a question in Wisconsin yesterday about President Rodham. The person asked did I continue to support him when he was impeached?

"Yes, I continued to support him, but not because he was a Democrat. I supported him because I don't believe cheating on your wife is a threat to national security. Yes, he lied under oath, but I believe he lied to keep his wife from finding out that he had sex in the Oval Office. What man wouldn't lie about that?"

A voice from the crowd yelled, "Jesus Christ!"

Yvonne replied, "None of us are Jesus Christ. But you can't place former President Rodham's actions in the same category as the actions of President Donaldson, who's guilty of bribery, abuse of power, obstruction of Congress and justice, and other high crimes and misdemeanors. If anyone says he is not, they are not honest with themselves.

"I can't speak for others, but if a Democrat did one-eighth of what President John Donaldson has done, I would be at the forefront for impeachment because I believe in country before party.

"Let me take you into history. President Lincoln, a Republican, freed the slaves. The Fourteenth Amendment in 1868 granted ex-slaves the rights of a citizen. Because Lincoln freed them, African Americans registered as Republicans but were systematically turned away from voting. To solve the injustice, in 1870 Congress passed the Fifteenth Amendment, which states that a citizen's right to vote shall not be denied. But states circumvented the Constitution to prevent blacks from voting. The main culprits were the Democrats in the Southern states, who charged African Americans a tax to vote, or gave literacy tests, or intimidated blacks to prevent them from voting.

"God raised up a prophet named Dr. Martin Luther King, who led the protests in the South. And in 1965, the Voting Rights Act, signed into law by President Johnson, a Democrat, prohibited states from using literacy tests and other methods to prevent blacks from voting.

"Blacks began registering by the hundreds of thousands as Democrats. That's when the George Wallace democrats left the party. Most of them joined the Republican party; others went back into the hills and to their farms and plantations.

"I want to speak to the black people for a minute. A lot of black men and women were killed fighting for our right to vote. We are obligated to vote by the blood that was shed by them. So, vote. What I often hear is that I don't want to vote for the lesser of two evils. Then vote for yourself. Write your own name on the ballot. What's important is that you vote! We need you to vote! We need every race of people to vote!

"Remove the excuses. Don't allow laziness, or the thought that your vote doesn't matter, lead you. If you embrace that thought, you will create an energy that will spread to others. And imagine when others embrace excuses that come from the feeling of laziness. They too will spread that lazy energy, and soon millions of people will make an excuse not to vote.

"There is power in our hands. It is the power to vote. If more people disagree with your vote, so be it. But the energy goes both ways. When you are determined to vote, you create an energy that motivates others to vote, and that energy spreads because enthusiasm gives birth to activism, and activism convinces others to participate.

"There is power in the people. The power is the right to vote. There are more good people than bad people in every state, like there are more good people than bad people in the world. So, what would the world look like if all the good people voted? Let's see that day come before Judgment Day."

A standing ovation followed as she left the podium.

The attendees surrounded Yvonne as if she were a political candidate. She ignored the reporters' questions, "Are you going to run for political office? Did you move to New York to run for the Senate? Are you setting yourself up to run for the presidency in 2024?"

In her steps to leave the venue, she noticed a woman in the crowd who was wearing a black and red sweatshirt that read, "Lewis College of Business—Founded in 1928." She stopped and shook the hand of the gray-haired woman.

"Can I take a selfie of us?" the woman asked.

"Of course," Yvonne replied.

After the picture, Yvonne said, "Did you attend Lewis?"

"Yes, I did," she proudly said. "Class of 1976. You know we were the first HBCU in Michigan?"

Yvonne smiled. "I didn't know that. Is the school still open?"

The woman's expression saddened. "The doors closed in 2013."

The reporters had their recorders and cameras on the conversation, and the woman said, "I hope you run for president?"

"I'm just using my energy to defeat Donaldson in next year's election. Besides, I'm not a politician. I'm just a businesswoman."

"Donaldson is a pitiful businessman, and he was elected. You are a successful businesswoman. You don't have to be a politician anymore to run for president. Think about running in 2024."

Yvonne smiled. "What is your name?"

"Hattie."

"Nice to meet you, Hattie." Yvonne reached into her pants pocket and handed her business card. "Please call me."

A minute later, social media had spread the rumor that Yvonne was running for president in 2024.

* * *

Charlene and Amari were chatting on Skype. Tunes by Khalid and Lucky Daye played in her background.

"You sure you want to marry me?" she asked out of the blue.

"Of course! Where did that question come from?"

She paused before she said, "What is marriage to you?"

He tilted his head. "I define marriage as two individuals living as one flesh. The pain and joy for one is pain and joy for the other. Living as one flesh doesn't mean that each individual must share all things in common, but the things that bring solace must be mutual in some way."

"I know the definition of solace, but what do you mean by it?"

"The solace I'm talking about is faith—not religion, but faith. If one believes in Jesus, but the other doesn't, there isn't any solace between them, because solace begins with faith. Marriage isn't changing who you are, but being comfortable with the other in your individuality. There will be different likes and dislikes—even the religion can be different—but the faith must be the same."

Amari paused.

"Keep going, I'm listening," she said.

"Every marriage faces trials and tribulations. That is the stress and anxiety caused by bills, job-related matters, and family issues. How one relieves their stress and anxiety may vary, but there has to be open communication between the mates. If not, one will feel the need for mental affection, which comes from the feeling of being heard and understood. If that doesn't exist in the marriage, one will seek it outside, and the temptation of adultery will increase, and an affair will inevitably occur. Communication prevents the mental space from occurring between mates, so your mate must be your best friend. And there shouldn't be any secrets. Do you have a secret that you haven't shared with me?"

"Do you have a secret that you haven't shared with me?" she asked him.

"You're answering a question with a question."

"Jesus did that often. The question is the answer. You are so much like Derrick. You keep secrets from the one you love. Why?"

"Why do you keep secrets from me?"

"How do you know that I have any secrets?"

"Because you said, the question to me is the answer to my question—and yes, I have secrets that I haven't shared with you."

"What's the reason? When you are engaged, you shouldn't have any more secrets," Charlene said angrily.

"I disagree. When I am married, I won't have any secrets. I will tell you all my secrets on our wedding night. I expect you to do the same?"

"I wanna know now. What if one of your secrets is something that can harm me?"

"Then it wouldn't be a secret because I would've told you. If I love you, I won't harm you."

"So, what kind of secret are you keeping from me that you cannot tell me until we are married?"

"The same kind you are keeping from me."

She paused. *Man, he is smart. That's why I love him.* "Okay, you win—I'll wait. Tell me more about marriage?"

Amari had a slight grin and love written in his eyes. After a few seconds, he said, "Physical affection is the act of love, but mental affection is the fullness of love. Many mistake sex for making love. But making love is the conversation after sex. If there is no desire to converse after sex, then the couple didn't make love."

Charlene tilted her head to the side and narrowed her eyes. "We haven't had sex, so we haven't made love?"

"I haven't ended your virginity, but we made love."

"You right. We did. I love you, Amari."

"And I love you."

"Tell me more about marriage."

"O-okay. Marriage requires the freedom of space if wanted."

"Freedom of space? What's that? You need space when you get tired of me?"

"No, it's not that. I'm saying that it shouldn't be a requirement for one to leave the house only in the company of the other. Trust and honesty are important because it kills insecurity. But if one's actions blemish the trust and honesty, the marriage might not recover its splendor, because of skepticism."

"How do you know so much about marriage, and you haven't been married? Or have you? Is that one of your secrets? Why are you in Toronto on Labor Day weekend?"

"You know why. I asked you to come with me."

"Yeah, but you knew I had to work this weekend. What hotel you at?"

"I'm not at a hotel. I'm staying with the Mother Sarah."

"Who's that? You staying at a woman's house?"

"She's fifty-nine years old and married. It's custom for the leader to spend the night at the home of the Mother Sarah when he visits the tabernacles. And no, I haven't been married before. I know about marriage from studying myself, because knowing one's self is the realization of others. I know the things that comfort and satisfy me, so I look for those things in a mate. I found them in you. Do you know what is the most important thing that mates must have in common?"

"Faith?"

"Nope. Friendship. We have to see each other as best friends. We have to see each other as ourselves. If I can see myself in you, and you can see yourself in me, then how can our marriage fail if we love and like each other?"

Charlene was pondering those words when he continued.

"There is a difference between loving someone and being in love. Love is care and concern, but being in love is the need and desire to spend the days of your life with that person. I'm in love with you, Charlene."

She leaked tears of joy.

Amari continued, "Marriage is falling in love over and over again. That is why you have to love and like each other. You won't continue falling in love if one doesn't like the other."

"I don't like the idea of falling in love over and over again. Why not stay in love when you fall in love?"

"Falling in love over and over again is how you stay in love. In marriage, there will be differences that lead to disagreements and arguments, which interferes with the feeling of being in love. If you like each other, the division will be minimal, because you will kiss and make up. That is falling in love again.

"See how important it is to not only love your mate but also like your mate? Some people love their mate but don't like them. Some like their mate but don't love them. Loneliness and gratitude are often mistaken for being in love. I believe most marriages don't last because one or both got married because of loneliness or gratitude and because one or both love their mate but don't like them, or stopped liking them."

"How can you love someone and not like them?"

"You can love a person for the way he or she treats you, or for the way he or she provides for you, but not like them because of their habits, attitude, beliefs, et cetera."

"I like you."

"And I like you."

"I love you."

"And I love you and will fall in love with you over and over again."

CHAPTER 12

The alt-right propaganda channel, XOF News, was reveling in Donaldson's acquittal and boasted that the president would win reelection.

Hornsby had his own Frank Gurtner as the attorney general who openly initiated investigations into Donaldson's political rivals to tarnish their reputations in the hope of dissuading voters from the candidates on the Left.

Donaldson's allies in Congress continued to defend his lies and block the quest for truth, which seemingly emboldened him. At his first rally after his acquittal, in Benito Mussolini style, Donaldson boldly said, "I have total authority." He received rousing applause from the forty thousand plus attendees when he said, "I will be President for twelve, maybe sixteen years."

After receiving harsh criticism from the media for the comments, Donaldson's allies in Congress and his pundits claimed he was joking. But in the middle of the night, Donaldson tweeted that he would be president for life.

The morning after that tweet, Hornsby summoned Donaldson to the VP office.

"Thank you, Mr. Hornsby, for your help. The Democrats should be charged with treason."

"In due time. But first, we have to get you reelected, and that requires a change."

"What kind of change?" he harshly asked.

"You are guilty of every article of impeachment sent to the Senate, and the ones not sent. The only reason you are still the president is because of me. I control your allies in Congress. You don't have any friends. The senator from South Carolina is your friend until I tell him not to be. You and your family are dead without me. So listen carefully. I am the boss. I want you to cancel all interviews except for XOF. On the campaign trail, read every word on the script given without adding or deleting. Don't say anything on the campaign trail that's not in the prepared stump speech."

The president leaned forward in the side chair and placed his arms on Hornsby's desk. "Why are you so disrespectful to me?"

"Take your body parts off my desk if you want to keep them."

The president quickly removed arms.

"I'm not disrespectful. Just honest. You're the emperor walking around with no clothes, and your subjects are saying how good you look in your clothes. As your VP, I am one of your subjects in the letter only. You serve me at my pleasure. Don't ever forget that."

Donaldson lowered his head. The bully he portrayed was a punk behind the mask.

"Raise your head! John, I'm your best friend. If I weren't, I would've let them convict you in the Senate. You can trust me."

"I was thinking that you became the vice-president to become president when Congress fired me."

"You see how stupid you were not to realize that I'm your best friend? If I wanted you removed, I wouldn't've bribed the Senate to acquit you. I became your VP to help you win reelection. We are running neck and neck in the polls with the presumed candidate. I need you to stay on the script until after the election. Don't tweet anything without my approval. I've told you that before."

Donaldson lowered his eyes like a scolded child. "I'm sorry. I will."

"I've heard that before. But you continue to disappoint your best friend by thinking you know better than me. After the election, you won't have to read another script, and you can tweet 24/7 if you like—say whatever you feel, do whatever you want, because you will be president for life."

Donaldson smiled. "I like that."

"But don't tell the world before the time. It's a surprise party."

The president chuckled.

* * *

Rhea-Toni was sitting on Derrick's lap. Three-year-old Malachi was watching cartoons on the stationed iPad. Anthony was asleep in the baby seat next to Juna, whose head was pressed on Derrick's upper arm. Charlene and Amari were watching the unreleased *Peb Falls* movie on the 4K screen.

As the private plane descended to the Cape Town airport, Derrick, Juna, and Charlene marveled at the scenic views around them.

Two chauffeured black SUVs, each with two assigned bodyguards in the front seats, drove them from the airport to the exclusive resort. The partly sunny sky and twenty-four-mile-per-hour wind greeted them as they departed the vehicles and stepped onto the gray stone pavers. The briny air carried their noses to the woodsy cedar and vanilla scent inside the boutique hotel. The music by Zim Ngqawana from the lobby's ceiling broadened their smiles.

Charlene and Amari entered the room on the first floor that had the plunge pool and sunbathing patio.

Derrick, Juna, and their children entered the deluxe suite on the top floor. The king-sized platform bed facing the ocean had three roomy playpens next to it.

Malachi waddled behind Derrick onto the private balcony with the ocean and mountain view. He lifted Malachi by the waist and swung him left and right. "Mister, this is South Africa."

The next day, accompanied by bodyguards, the group rode the cableway to the top of Table Mountain. Against Juna's will, Derrick stood at the edge of the flat-topped mountain overlooking the city of Cape Town and lifted Rhea-Toni to face the sun as if presenting her before the eyes of God. After, he did the same with Malachi and Anthony.

"Why did you do that?" Charlene asked. "Are you worshipping the sun now?"

Holding Malachi's right hand, Derrick cracked a smile. "It's written in the book of Malachi, 'But unto you that fear my name shall the Sun (S-u-n) of righteousness arise with healing in his wings; and ye shall go forth, and grow up as calves of the stall.'" (Malachi 4:2)

"Isn't that a typo? I think it was meant to be S-o-n." She looked at Amari. "What do you think?"

Amari said, "The Bible is the word of God, and God is perfect, so there isn't an error in the Bible."

With her eyes in the neutral position, Charlene said, "Show me another Scripture."

Juna was rocking Anthony to sleep in her arms. Her daughter sat quietly in the three-seat stroller.

Derrick said, "One Scripture is enough. A lot of people believe the Bible contradicts itself and that scrolls are missing. But as Amari said, God is perfect. There aren't any missing scrolls for the Bible, and there aren't any errors, just an understanding some don't have."

Charlene shifted her eyes back to Amari. "Okay, so give me an understanding of the s-u-n of righteousness."

Amari said, "Psalm 84:11, says, 'For the Lord God is a sun and shield; the Lord will give grace and glory. No good thing will he withhold from them that walk uprightly.' According to that Scripture, God is a s-u-n."

"But is God the sun?" Charlene asked with her debating voice.

"I don't think Derrick was saying God is the sun."

Derrick intervened, "Charlene, I don't believe God is the sun. But there is a 'Sun of righteousness,' and that is the light of Jesus Christ. In chapter one of Revelation, verses 13-18, those Scriptures describe one like unto the Son of man. Verse 16 says, '...and his countenance was as the sun shineth in his strength.'"

Juna interjected, "Stop debating. Let's go and have fun."

With a satisfied pout, Charlene said, "Okay."

Derrick led their steps to the cableway with Malachi beside him.

Juna set Anthony next to Rhea-Toni and pushed the stroller.

Amari followed with his arm around Charlene's shoulders. Her head leaned on his.

Two bodyguards walked in the front and two behind at all times in their travel and tour of the Kirstenbosch Gardens that ended with dinner and entertainment at the Victoria & Alfred Waterfront.

* * *

While her children were in South Africa, Yvonne was in Chicago for a political event and boarded the L train for the experience. The ride passed homes that she could almost touch if the windows were open.

Two teens boarded at the fourth stop. Both wore oversized black jackets with hoods trimmed with fake fur, baggy jeans, and untied buff-colored boots.

As they walked toward where Yvonne was sitting, the elderly white woman who sat across from her on the other side of the aisle, clutched her purse against her.

The shorter of the two teens looked at the woman and smiled. "All black teens aren't thieves," he said, and the two sat facing Yvonne.

Frowning, the elderly white woman turned toward the window without relaxing her grip on her purse.

Yvonne smiled at the teens. "Hi. How are you?"

"It's all good," they replied simultaneously.

"Shouldn't you be in school?"

The shorter one said, "We're high school seniors. We only have two morning classes on Wednesdays."

"You must be honor students."

The taller one broke his silence. "We are."

"Congratulations! So where are you all headed?"

The taller one said, "You mean college or now?"

"Now."

"The soup kitchen."

"We help to feed the homeless on Wednesdays," the shorter one said.

Yvonne's smile broadened. "I'm impressed. Are you registered to vote?"

"I am," the shorter one said.

"I'll be eighteen in March," the taller one replied.

"Are you going to vote?"

"No doubt," they both answered.

Then the shorter one said, "We can't let that racist win again."

Yvonne nodded and asked, "What college are you attending?"

The shorter one said, "I'm going to Texas Southern."

"Prairie View," the taller one said. "This is our stop. Nice to meet you, lady. Peace out," the taller one said.

"Stay safe," the other said.

"Thank you. Stay safe," she replied.

As the train continued, Yvonne's instincts led her to exit at the Riverdale community. She googled the area and surprisingly learned that Derrick had built a charter school inside that community. Like a tourist, she was walking and found herself at the Altgeld Gardens housing project, where she approached a group of young men whose faces were hidden by their hooded coats.

"Hello. I'm looking for the Unity Corporation charter school?"

Three of the five turned around. The other two lifted their heads. One pointed the direction. "It's on 137th Street."

"Can I ask a question?"

"Yeah," several said simultaneously.

"Is the Unity Corporation helping this neighborhood?"

"Yeah," they all said.

"How is it helping?"

The seemingly oldest, who had the tattoo on his neck that appeared to come from his chest, said, "That school gives the kids hope. If that school was here when I was a teen, I wouldn't've been gangbanging."

Another said, "I couldn't find a job when I got out the joint, but I got hired by the Unity Corporation superstore on 121st. I work the midnight shift."

The youngest-looking one said, "I work there too. I'm off today."

Yvonne shifted her eyes back to the oldest. "Are you still gangbanging?"

"Gangbanging was the only life we had around here. But things are changed now that we have black-owned stores in the community that are hiring people from the community."

Yvonne said, "That's good to hear, but you haven't answered my question?"

He ran the side of his finger under his nose. "Nah, I'm not gangbanging."

"Are you working?"

"I work at the superstore too, from 2 p.m. to 10 p.m. I gotta get ready to bounce for work."

"One last question: Do you vote?"

"Nah. But I would've voted for the black president if I wasn't locked up."

The others said, "I voted for the black president."

"Are you going to vote next year?"

Three were silent, and two said, "I doubt it."

"I need you all to vote. You know we got to get the president up out of there. But I need you to vote in the local elections too. Have you seen the need-to-vote commercials?"

"Yeah, we saw the commercials," one said.

"Did the commercials make you want to vote?"

"At the time, it did."

"What about now?"

"I'm not feeling it right now. The election is a year away."

"It is, but you have to start talking about it now. Black candidates are running for mayor and city council. Vote if you like one of them."

"I'm down with the Unity Corporation, but they haven't endorsed a candidate yet."

"That's why I'm in Chicago, to endorse the candidates running for the Senate, House of Representatives, mayor, state and city legislators."

"You work for the Unity Corporation?"

"I do."

"That's what's up. But the only important vote is for president."

"The local elections are important also," she said. "Those are the ones that have an immediate impact on your community. Those are the ones that can block the Unity Corporation from being in your community if the wrong people get elected."

"For real?"

"Yeah. I need you all to vote. It's very important. We can change the world if we vote."

"What's your name?"

"Yvonne Dunbar. Derrick Williams is my son."

"Ohhh snap! Really? Word! That's what's up!" spewed from their mouths.

The oldest one said, "I knew you were someone important."

"We all are important. You are important, and everyone in this community is important. I need you all to help."

"What you need?" they all eagerly said.

"I need you to vote and get your family and friends to vote. I need you to help get everybody who is eighteen and older to vote."

"Yeah, alright, bet," were their replies.

"There are incentives too."

She had their attention. She opened her phone, tapped one of the apps, and scrolled down.

She raised her head. "We are sponsoring a concert in Lincoln Park next summer and the only way you can get a ticket is to collect enough volunteer points from registering new voters, making phone calls, passing out flyers, and community service."

The youngest said, "You can't buy a ticket?"

She shook her head. "Nope."

"What artists gonna be there?" another asked.

"Travis Scott is one."

"Travis Scott!"

She peeked at her phone. "Yes, and Kodak Black and others."

"Kodak Black! That's one hundred!"

She opened her purse and handed each a business card. "Call that number for information on how to register as a volunteer."

"Word, bet, I'm down, and thanks," came from their mouths.

Yvonne smiled, shook the hand of each, and waved as she left. The pleasant encounters on the subway and at the public housing complex carried her thoughts to the sight of the Black

Liberation flag hanging from the school's ivory brick structure.

Eager to escape the cold, she ran up the sandstone steps and entered the middle of the three doors. After passing through the metal detector, one of the two armed security guards escorted her to the principal's office.

The door was open, and when she entered, the principal quickly stood wide-eyed and open-mouthed. His oval face with a five-o'clock shadow had a broad smile, which she found attractive. He smiled broadly and hurried around his desk, hand extended to her.

"Hi, Mrs. Dunbar. This is a pleasant surprise. Welcome."

She shook his hand. "Thank you. I'm surprised that you know my name. Have we met before?"

"We have not, but I watch the news. I'm honored to have you as a visitor. Can I give you a tour?"

"I would love that if you're not busy."

"I'm busy, but not too busy to give you a tour."

She smiled and he returned the smile.

During the tour, she caught his seemingly flirtatious glances at her, and she didn't mind them. The tour that ended at the modest-sized health suite where the nurse and certified assistant, both in white lab coats were on duty.

Two boys lay on the three cots.

"What happened to them?" Yvonne asked.

"One has a stomachache, and the other has a headache."

"Are those the typical symptoms that bring the kids in here?"

"Sometimes a child will fall on the playground and scrape a knee or have an injury in the gym, but we also have kids who come in to talk about their homes and bodies. We also have a mental health counselor on staff. When we discover signs of abuse and mental abnormality, we notify the authorities."

"Does that happen often?"

"More than it should."

Yvonne's raised her brows, and the principal asked, "Are you ready to go?"

She remembered what had happened to Derrick. Apparently noticing that something bothered her, the principal led her into the vacant hallway where tan lockers on each side stretched along the well-lit corridor.

"When are you returning to New York?" he asked as they slowly walked side by side toward the building's exit.

She smiled with the sense of the next question and halted. She lifted the phone from her purse and dialed a cab.

The principal stopped.

After she ended the call, she turned to face him. "I'm scheduled to return tomorrow. Why?"

"Because I'm not ready to leave your company."

"Ah. So, what are you proposing?"

"Dinner tonight?"

"Umm. Okay."

"Great. I know a nice place where we can eat some soul food and listen to live jazz."

"I like that."

"Is eight o'clock good for you, or is that too late?"

"I usually don't eat dinner that late, but for you, I will make the exception."

His smile broadened, and they exchanged contact information.

"If you hadn't asked before I left this building, later would've been too late," Yvonne said.

"Oh? I couldn't've asked outside?"

"You could've asked, but I wouldn't've given my number."

"Why?"

"Because when I open the door of opportunity and the man hesitates to enter, that tells me that he is insecure. I like the confident man."

He clasped his hands with thumbs upright under his bottom lip. "The Bible says, 'Cast not away therefore your confidence, which hath great recompence of reward.'" (Hebrews 10:35)

"So, what is the meaning of that Scripture?"

"You said if I hadn't shown confidence, you wouldn't've given me a chance. I have endured many lonely days and nights, but I never lost my confidence. I see you as a reward for not losing my confidence."

"Wow. You move fast. We just met, and I'm your reward? Scary."

"Scary? Why? Time waits for no one. What I'm thinking now, I might not be able to say later. So, I'm saying it now."

She wanted to know more about this man. As if reading her thoughts, he said, "I want to get to know you too. I'm looking forward to dinner tonight."

"Oh, so you're a mind reader? You know what I'm thinking?"

"I'm hoping that we are thinking the same."

She smiled and continued down the hall. The sound of her three-inch heels on the floor echoed down the hall. He stayed at her side, silent.

They exited through the door she had entered.

"It's freezing out here," she said. "You better get back inside. You don't have a coat on."

He grinned and didn't appear bothered by the frigid temperature.

"I'm okay. You don't have to wait. The cab will be here in a minute or two."

"I want to wait."

"I got a coat on, and I'm still cold. I know you don't want to catch a cold, because if you do, I'm canceling our date tonight. I don't want you spreading your germs to me." She chuckled.

Before he could reply, the cab arrived, and he raced down the steps to the curb as if he could outrun the bites from the cold.

He was noticeably shivering when he opened the door. She smiled and quickly got in. They waved at each other as he hurried back up the steps.

She watched him enter the building as the cab drove away. She contemplated, staring out the backseat window, seeing one thing and thinking of another.

In the fourth rewind of her scenes with the principal, she entered the hotel room that overlooked Lake Michigan. She stood at the picture window that faced the bed, pondering her many thoughts while listening to the voice of Sade from her iPhone docking station on the dresser.

She stayed at the window until darkness had replaced the sunset. A song by Lonette McKee was playing as she entered the shower without closing the curtains. The lyrics, "At least I had you one time," brought the teardrop of memory that reflected in the nearly steam-covered bathroom mirror. She stared at her expression. *Cedric, I can see you in him.*

* * *

Dressed in the charcoal-check dress with peplum waist detail, Yvonne slipped black heels over her sheer, black pantyhose.

She faced the mirror and turned sideways. She pouted at the small bulge that previously was unimportant and tried to suck-it-in. *I need to lose weight.* With time to spare, she sat on the chair that was catercorner to the bed and called Charlene on FaceTime.

"How do I look?"

"Nice. Where are you going?"

Yvonne stood and looked sideways in the mirror. "My tummy big?"

"Your tummy isn't big. My tummy is big. Where are you going?"

"I have a date."

Charlene smiled. "What! Who? Aren't you in Chicago?"

"Yes, I'm in Chicago. I met him at Derrick's charter school. He's the principal."

"What's his name?"

"Terrance."

"How old is he?"

"Fifty-five."

"He has children?"

"He has two girls."

"How old?"

"I don't know. I didn't ask."

"Hmm. Was he married before?"

"Yes."

"How long ago?"

"Six years."

"How long was he married?"

"Twenty-two years."

"He got divorced after twenty-two years? He must have cheated on his wife."

"Nope. She was one of the teachers killed at that school shooting in Minnesota."

"Oh. Sorry. I remember that. So sad. How long has he been living in Chicago?"

"Since March. He moved here when he got the job."

"You sound happy, Ma. He must be special."

"He's nice. It's just a date."

"Ma, I know you. I haven't heard you sound like this before."

"Sound like what? I'm just answering your questions."

"It's not what you say but how you say it. Sound gives sight. I can see the hidden excitement in your voice. I'm happy for you, Ma."

"Thank you, but it's only a date. I live in New York, and he lives in Chicago. That says it all."

"No, it doesn't. You can move to Chicago, or he can move to New York."

"I wouldn't want him to move. He has an important job that he loves."

"So, you move. You can work anywhere in the U.S."

"This is something I shouldn't be thinking about right now. It's only the first date. I'm still getting to know him, and he's still getting to know me. We might not have enough things in common."

"Didn't you teach me to think ahead? To always be prepared for the what-if?"

"As an expression," Yvonne answered before she said, "I have to get ready to go."

"Okay, Ma. Have fun."

Yvonne smiled. "Thanks. I love you."

"And I love you, Mama. Call me when you back. I'll wait up. I want to hear everything."

"You might be waiting all night."

"I better not be."

"I'm just kidding. I'll call you."

"You better."

"Now, who's acting like the parent?"

Charlene chuckled. "I'm sorry, Ma. But you know I got to look out for you."

"I'll call you when I get back."

"Thanks."

With her emotions captured by the voice of Aretha Franklin, Yvonne sat on the edge of the bed. When the Teddy Pendergrass song "Somebody Told Me" came on, she turned her head slowly to face the mirror.

She sang as she applied the brown-nude lipstick that matched her nails. She wrapped herself and left the room determined to follow the advice of the song's lyrics to submit to the master plan.

When Yvonne entered the restaurant/jazz club on State Street, Terrance was waiting at the maître d' station. His stylish dark suit and white three-peak hanky highlighted his debonair appearance.

She smiled.

He smiled back and stepped toward her. His fresh-scented cologne wafted into the brief embrace. "You look stunning," he said as patrons walked around them.

After several seconds, they turned to the maître d', who was patiently standing in his black tuxedo. With an ostrich walk, he led them to the left front of the stage and seated them at a two-person table. The soft music from overhead added to the tranquil atmosphere.

Both ordered the seafood dinner. Afterward, Yvonne ordered the glass of white wine, and Terrance ordered bourbon. Their chat, centered on their personal histories, stretched into politics and religion. As if on cue, the lights dimmed when their drinks were at their mouths, and applause replaced the indistinct conversations around them.

The saxophone player opened with his solo, followed by the infusion from the drummer, keyboardist, and bass. The ending of the fifty-minute performance was like the beginning and concluded with a standing ovation that Yvonne and Terrance joined.

The lights returned, and Terrance lifted Yvonne's gray sheepskin coat off the back of her chair and held it so she could slide her arms inside. He whispered into her ear, "Thank you for coming," and draped the coat over her shoulders.

She fastened the buttons, then put on her black leather gloves and faced him.

His eyes were staring into hers. After he put on his black wool coat and gloves, he led her by the hand across the street to the lake. With their hands on the railing, they stared at the crescent moon and its reflection in dark waters below.

"Life has so much beauty, in the day and at night," she said.

"What is life to you?" he asked.

She turned to him. "Of course, life is God. But life is also mirrored."

"Mirrored?"

"Yes. When we look in the mirror, we see our flesh only. When God looks at us in the mirror, He sees our hearts and intentions. He sees and knows the things we hide from others. Mirrors are objects of specular reflection. That includes the reflection of ourselves. People see God differently when they look into the mirror of their minds. Some see God as black, some as white, some as he, some as she; some see God as a thing, some see God as a place, some see God as a myth."

"How do you see God?"

"I see God in all good people. They show their faith by their works."

"Amen."

She smiled sideways. "What time is it?"

He lifted his left wrist and looked at his silver watch. "Ten thirty-seven. Are you ready for the date to end?"

She slowly rocked side-to-side. "No. But you got a school to run in the morning."

"I also have a personal life to live. I can do both."

"Sounds like you're not ready for me to leave."

"Now that I found you, I'm not. But this is only the beginning."

"What is the end?"

"This is the beginning without end."

She studied him. *I like him.*

"I like you too."

"How did you know what I was thinking?"

"I didn't. But I guessed right."

He seized the moment and kissed her, and she returned the passion.

"I can drive you back to your hotel."

"No, I'll take the cab."

"Why?"

"Because one thing will lead to another, and I'm not ready for that."

"Okay. I understand."

"Thank you."

They kissed again, longer than the first time.

She dodged the third kiss as she entered the cab. "That's enough for the night. Nothing personal." She smiled cleverly.

Terrace stood expressionless as he watched the cab drive away.

CHAPTER 13

The phone rang.
"Hello," Yvonne muttered.
"Good morning."
"Terrance?"
"Yes. You don't recognize my voice?"
"Umm, what time is it?"
"Seven."
"Why are you calling so early?"
"First, I was thinking about you. Second, I will probably be too busy to speak with you once school starts. I was hoping you would be happy to hear my voice, but you sound a little agitated."
"I'm not. I'm happy to hear your voice, just surprised that you called so early."
"I'm sorry. I'll let you go back to sleep."
"It's okay. I'm up now. Are you in the office?"
"I am. I'm calling because I want to see you before you go back tomorrow."
"You could've called later to ask that?"
"Might've been too late. There are a lot of men in Chicago looking for a woman like you."
She felt herself blush. "What happened to that confident man that I saw last night? Does absence make you insecure?"
"Not at all. I remain confident, but not overconfident, because that leads to taking things for granted, and I will never take you for granted."
"Oh, so I'm a thing?"
"I was speaking in the informal term."
She giggled. "I know. Just messing with you. I'm happy to hear that you won't take me for granted."
"A wise man takes nothing for granted."
Yvonne's eyes narrowed in thought before she said, "I think I'll stay in Chicago, a little longer."

* * *

Eleven weeks had passed since their first meeting, and Yvonne and Terrance spent the weekends together. Either she was in Chicago, or he joined her when she was traveling. The last weekend in January, they were in the Bahamas.

Yvonne's long fingers were scrapping the white sand as she and Terrance lay silently on white chaise lounges in-between two tall palm trees. Their eyes, covered with fashionable sunglasses, faced the overhanging leaves that partially blocked the sun. In the background, the ocean was splashing onto the shore.

"Are we at a dead end?" Yvonne said.

He turned quickly to her. "What? A dead end? Where did that come from?"

"You're not talking," she said. "Is this our last weekend together?"

He removed his sunglasses and sat up, facing her. His brown crisscross sandals sunk into the sand. He hung his shades on the closed top button of his tangerine linen shirt. His forehead wrinkled. "I was only thinking."

"I could feel that you were thinking, but about what? I'm thinking that you're ready to move on."

"Now you sound like the one who's insecure."

"No, I'm not. I'm just feeling your vibes. You're the one who was always talking, and now you're not. Why?"

"I don't know what to say. I can't say what's on my mind because you said I'm moving too fast. So instead of just talking to be talking, I'm keeping my thoughts to myself. I'm following your lead."

She quickly sat up. Her bare feet sank into the warm sand. She removed her shades, gripped the side of the lounger with both hands, and leaned forward. "What is it that you want to say?"

He didn't hesitate. "We've been together every day in one way or another for three months. I'm not trying to wait another three months before we go to the next level. I love you, Yvonne. I'm not a kid. I know what love is. I want us to get married."

"Married? We've only known each other for three months. Aren't you happy with the way things are?"

"No. I'm fifty-six. I don't want a girlfriend. I want a wife to grow old with."

"Terrance, I can see myself marrying you one day. But you know how busy I am. Right now, I can't be the wife you want."

"The wife I want? What do you think I want in a wife?"

She leaned back slightly.

"Yvonne, I see marriage as two people living as one flesh in the same spirit. That doesn't mean we have to be together in the flesh at all times. Because if we're together in spirit, then we're together in the flesh, even if we're on different continents."

Her eyes narrowed.

He continued, "If we're connected spiritually, then we're connected mentally, so we can feel each other's thoughts even when we're out of each other's sight. I know you can feel my thoughts when we're not together. I can feel yours. I'm ready to move to the next level because I know what true love is. I'm not mistaking loneliness for love. I know the values that I need in a wife. I'm not at a dead end. I'm on the next level, waiting for you to join me. Don't tell me it's too soon. It wasn't too soon to accept Cedric's ring. Your son married his wife after a month. Look at how happy they are! Why waste time when you know what love is?"

Yvonne pondered that while slowly rubbing her thighs with her polished nails. "I love you, Terrance. I can see myself as your wife. But I think you're looking for more than I can give. My priority is the get-out-the-vote project. The presidential election is nine months away. You know that I will be traveling almost every day until the election."

"That doesn't bother me. The school is my priority. Like you, I'm on the front line of this fight. But when I take a rest, I want my other half to be there, if only by phone. God brought you into my life because I prayed for a woman like you. If I become ill, I expect to be your priority. If you become ill, you will be my priority. Other than that, your priority at this time should be your project, like mine is the school."

With tears at the edge and outstretched arms, she softly said, "Come here."

He embraced and initiated their passionate kiss.

***

BREAKING NEWS: "There was a shooting tonight at the Unity Corporation movie theater in Langston, Oklahoma. Several reportedly are killed and wounded. The shooter was shot and killed by the security guard.

"The gunman hasn't been identified but is reported to be a white male. The police are searching the pickup truck parked in front of the theater behind me. As you can imagine, it is a very chaotic scene here. I am Shelly Hill, reporting for NCC, in Langston, Oklahoma."

The anchors were discussing the shooting when they suddenly returned to the reporter.

"I'm with Shawntae Phillips. Shawntae, tell us what you witnessed?"

Her trembling voice said, "We were watching Peb Falls when we heard shots. People started screaming and hiding on the floor. I didn't move for some reason. I looked in the direction of the shots and saw the back of a man in dark clothing and a red hat. He was spraying bullets with a rifle. I was frozen in my seat. I couldn't turn away. Then the security guard shot him."

"What happened after that?"

"I don't know. My friends grabbed my arms and led me outside."

"Thank you, Shawntae."

"You're welcome."

"We can report that four people are confirmed dead and nine wounded. The casualties would've been much higher if the security guard wasn't present. I spoke to the representative for the Unity Corporation, who told me that all of their movie theaters, schools, and stores have at least one armed security guard on duty at all times. No one expected this type of violence to occur in Langston, one of the thirteen historic all-black towns that still exist in Oklahoma. I am Shelly Hill reporting for NCC."

The next day, Derrick, Xavier, and Gladys arrived in Langston to visit the families of those who were killed and wounded. The following day, without the presence of bodyguards, the Unity Corporation held a news conference outside the theater in Langston.

Derrick stood at the lectern in his black full-length cashmere coat and black-speckled cuffed beanie. Xavier stood on one side and Gladys on the other.

"I'm here today to support those who were mercilessly killed and wounded by hate. The Unity Corporation will cover all expenses that exceed their life and medical insurance. I want to thank the security guard for his bravery to face an AR-15 with his revolver. He is a hero and deserving of a hero's reward. His spirit shows that we are not afraid and will risk our lives to save others. Any questions?"

Hands raised quickly. Derrick pointed at the white female reporter.

"Mr. Williams. Are you afraid of future attacks on your properties? And what are you going to do to prevent future attacks?"

"As I just stated, we are not afraid, as a community or individuals. As for prevention, we can only set up guard rails that include armed security, which we currently have on all of our properties. Next question?"

A white male reporter asked, "What do you say to those who believe you are dividing the country into whites and nonwhites?"

"How am I dividing the country into whites and nonwhites when, as a nonwhite, I have white teachers and principals in some of my schools and white managers in some of my stores? Economically empowering black communities shouldn't be seen as dividing the country the same as economically empowering white, Asian, and Jewish communities aren't seen as dividing the country. Racism is dividing the country. Next question."

"Mr. Williams, what do you want America to look like in the future?" a black male reporter asked.

"A country without hate. If you do not like white people, or black people, or Asians, or Jews, or Hispanics, or Indians, or the LBGTQ community, you don't have to socialize with them. But don't hate them to cause harm.

"During the Olympics, we don't care about the athletes' race or sexuality. We are rooting for the flag on the uniform. We are all Americans, and our diversity makes us stronger.

"Those who don't like their son or daughter to mingle outside their race shouldn't hate their son or daughter if they do, nor should they hate the person or persons that their son or daughter chooses to socialize with.

"If there are those who want to segregate themselves, let it be, but do not bring harm to those who don't. I believe in Judgment Day, and on that day, God will judge everyone, not by their race, or nationality, or religion, or sexual preference, but by their heart. Hopefully, America will become a country like that before Judgment Day."

* * *

Derrick, Xavier, and Gladys flew to Birmingham, Alabama. The driver of the rented black SUV greeted them when they exited the arrival gate. A fierce-looking man dressed in a black suit, white shirt, and black tie that matched the driver's clothing was standing outside the passenger's front door with a black briefcase in hand. He handed it to Xavier and opened the rear passenger's door. Xavier entered, followed by Gladys and Derrick. The man closed the door and sat at the front.

Xavier opened the case, three black 9mms were inside, each with an additional clip. He closed the case, placed it under the seat, and chatted with his wife and Derrick.

Several minutes later, the SUV pulled into the reserved parking space in front of the city hall. The three entered the building, with Gladys in the middle. After they had passed through security, an aide greeted and escorted them to the mayor's office.

The young black mayor was one of the stark supporters for the Unity Corporation and had given Derrick the key to the city.

The business meeting included dinner in the mayor's office and lasted for three hours. The four then rode with the mayor and his security team to watch the Unity Corporation Youth Choir perform at the landmark Alabama Theater.

When they returned to City Hall, the four stood on the sidewalk in front of the building and chatted amid the bustling sound of buses and rolling trucks. Handshakes ended the two-minute conversation.

Escorted by members of his security team, the mayor entered the building. Xavier, Gladys, and Derrick entered the SUV. Through the bulletproof windows, they saw crowds of pedestrians and bumper-to-bumper traffic as the vehicle headed to the hotel.

With the possibility of an assassin-in-wait at the forefront of their minds, Xavier lifted the case from under the seat and handed Gladys and Derrick each one of the loaded guns and extra clips. The dark-tinted windows blocked their actions from outside eyes.

Moments later, the vehicle entered the hotel's circular driveway and stopped in front of the gold-plated revolving glass entrance that had an automatic door on each side. The bellhop approached, but he was waved back by the man in the front passenger's seat, who had quickly opened his door.

The man in black looked around before he opened the rear door. The driver was unloading the three suitcases that he had placed in the trunk.

Derrick was the first to exit the vehicle, with his gun concealed.

The bellhop stood to the side with admiration in his eyes. "Welcome, Mr. Williams."

Derrick smiled, nodded, and handed him a twenty-dollar tip. Gladys and Xavier gave the same.

With their four-wheeled suitcases in hand, they followed the man in black to the check-in desk. The driver watched their backs.

After they had checked in, the three entered the dimly lit lounge and targeted the beige sofa at the back that faced the lounge's entrance. Watching everyone inside and entering, they ordered drinks and chatted.

"The mayor is very sharp," Gladys said.

"Yes, he is," Derrick replied.

"We need him as the governor."

"Has there been a black governor in Alabama?" he asked.

"No."

"Let's turn it blue."

She cracked a smile. "That's possible."

Xavier kept his eyes locked on the lounge entrance, with his right hand at the ready.

Derrick shifted to him. "Relax, we're safe."

"I'm relaxed, but we are not safe. The shooting in Langston is only the beginning. Lone wolves will continue to target our communities, but professional assassins will target us."

"I feel you, but I don't see them coming after you and Gladys. I'm the one they want out of the way."

Derrick eyed his untouched drink. He picked it up and set it down without a sip.

Xavier didn't sip his drink and kept his eyes locked on the entrance.

After Gladys had finished the remainder of her bottled water, she ended their silence. "I'm going to bed."

"I'm going with you," Xavier said.

"I'm going to stay here a little longer," Derrick said. "Goodnight. See you in the morning."

Xavier whispered in his ear, "Keep your eyes on the entrance, and take the stairs to your room."

Derrick nodded and stood. He and Xavier dapped before he kissed Gladys' cheek. He sat and watched until they left his sight, music by Petit Biscuit pictured the moment alone as he combatted the feelings of worry and fear.

CHAPTER 14

Charlene had opened a private office in South Philadelphia for her post-surgery patients. Inside her Center City duplex condo, songs by Alicia Keys played while she waited for Amari to arrive.

She was pouting. "He's always late. I should eat without him."

She called him, but his phone was off and her suspicions grew. Minutes later, there was a familiar knock, and she hesitantly opened the door.

"I'm sorry that I'm late," Amari said.

Charlene huffed, turned her back, and plopped on the gray linen chair at the glass dining table lit by two six-inch white candles.

"I'm sorry, I'm late," he said as he sat in the chair at her side. "I love the romantic atmosphere. I'm sorry, baby. I didn't want to spoil the evening for you."

She pouted and looked at the skyline view from the floor-to-ceiling open windows. Three seconds later, she faced him. "You are always late; Derrick is never late."

"I'm not Derrick! I need you to stop comparing me to Derrick."

"Shut up and eat. The food is getting cold."

"We need to talk about this. You keep comparing me to Derrick. I'm tired of hearing, 'Derrick would've done or said the same thing,' and 'Derrick would not have done or said that.' I'm not Derrick, and I don't want to be Derrick. He is his own man like I am my own man. We have a lot in common, but I'm not him."

"What are you saying? I know you're not him. But you remind me of him. I fell in love with you because you are a man like him."

"Are you in love with your brother?"

"Of course not. But I love him. I measure men by him. He's the type of man that I want to marry. I see him in you."

"That's the problem. You shouldn't see him in me. You should see me."

"I see you. I just said it wrong."

"I don't think you did. You said it the way you meant it. Before we got engaged, you weren't mentioning Derrick to me. But since we got engaged, that's all you do."

"No, it's not."

"Yes, it is. You don't realize how often you say it."

"I don't think there is a problem wanting a man like my brother. He is smart, spiritual, handsome, and devoted to his wife. I see all that in you, but I don't like it when you are late and don't call."

"So, you think I'm cheating on you?"

"Are you?" she shouted with her eyes wide.

"Oh my God, you think I'm seeing another woman. Charlene, I love you. I'm not interested in another woman. You know our lives are mirrored. God is watching everything we do. That's why we reap what we sow."

She lowered her head, ashamed, and muttered, "I'm sorry."

He embraced her. "I'm sorry for not calling. I didn't want the cell tower to trace my location. That's why I turned off my phone and removed the SIM card."

"Is that one of your secrets that I won't know until our wedding night?"

He sighed with his eyes locked on hers. "I'm gonna tell you now because I love you that much. The church has a storage place in every city, town, and village where our members reside."

"Storage? What type of storage?"

"Food, water, clothing, first-aid kits, toilet paper, and other basic needs."

"What for?"

"I've told you several times that we are living in the days of Revelation. It's only a matter of time for the beast to rise."

He opened his phone, tapped the app, and said, "Revelation 13:15-17 'And he hath power to give life unto the image of the beast, that the image of the beast should both speak, and cause that as many as would not worship the image of the beast should be killed. And he causeth all, both small and great, rich and poor, free and bond, to receive a mark in their right hand, or in their foreheads, and that no man might buy or sell, save he that had the mark, or the name of the beast, or the number of his name.'"

Charlene was silent in her thoughts but wanted to hear more.

"We believe there will be a new currency that only those who worship the beast will receive, so we will not be able to buy food and water unless we worship the beast. We do not know when that day will come, but we know the signs. That's why we are storing food kits that can stay fresh up to twenty-five years, and water, and clothing, and other needs."

She hissed. "Why couldn't you tell me this before?"

"I only have two secrets. I wanted to tell both on our wedding night."

She anxiously asked, "What's the other secret?"

"Our hiding place. That one will wait until our wedding night. Now tell me one of your secrets?"

"What?"

"It's March. We're getting married in August, and you haven't put your condo on the market."

"I will. You want me to move in with you before we get married."

"I do. But I don't want you coming back here after we get married."

"Why? What's wrong with that? Maybe I should keep it just in case you act up."

"Aha, So that's your plan. To keep it in case our marriage doesn't work out? That's the wrong mindset to take into the marriage."

"That's not my mindset, but you know how you men are?"

"No, how are we?"

"All lovey-dovey, and then after a year of marriage, the thrill is gone."

"Who told you that?"

"I've been talking to women."

"You can't generalize all men that way. You say you measure men by Derrick. Look at his marriage?"

"Yeah, but you're not Derrick. I've seen how those women in your church look at you. They are gritting on me, but you don't see it. I feel like an outsider because I haven't joined your church."

"I didn't ask you to join. You said you wanted to join."

"I said that 'cause I know you want me to join. We wouldn't've gotten engaged if I didn't say that."

"Sooo, you told me something that you don't mean? You lied to me?"

"No, I didn't. I meant it at the time. I'm just having second thoughts."

"That means you are having second thoughts about marrying me."

"No. I love you, Amari. I really do. I'm just scared. I've told you about the bad experiences I had."

"Charlene, we all had bad experiences in our life. But you cannot allow bad experiences to dictate your life going forward. What if you are operating on a patient and the patient dies? That's a bad experience. But you can't let that experience keep you from operating again. You remember the lesson in medical school, when the surgeon didn't save the patient? What did the surgeon do?"

"He lamented but continued his practice."

"That's right. There are things beyond our control, things we cannot prevent, and things that occur to discourage us and remove our trust. Please don't let a bad experience that didn't come from my actions remove your trust in me. Feel me?"

Charlene felt the sting of guilt. "I'm sorry. You're right. I like your church despite the women that are gritting. But I'm a surgeon. I have to work most Saturdays. What will the members think of you if your wife is working on the Sabbath? I don't want to be the cause for them to call your leadership into question."

"We've talked about this before. Not all of our members work Monday through Friday. Some jobs require them to work on Saturdays. But they make sure they are on leave for the seven days of Passover. Moreover, Jesus said it's not unlawful to do good and save life on the Sabbath day. You are a surgeon, so you are saving lives."

She placed her arms around him and her head on his shoulder. "You're right. I'm sorry. I shouldn't be wavering about joining your church. Baby, forgive me."

He tightened the embrace. "I love you, Charlene."

"I love you too."

They kissed with the passion that almost ended her virginity. The remix of the 2019 tune by Robyn played in the background.

* * *

Yvonne was in her bedroom. She had recently ended her daily video chat with Terrance when her cell rang. She looked at the caller ID and quickly answered. The crying voice said, "M-Mrs. D-Dunbar, Quelle is dead."

"What! What happened?"

"He was found in the woods."

"Oh my God!" She lowered her head and sobbed.

After several seconds, she lifted her head and sniffled. "Jermara, how did he die?"

"The police haven't said."

"What did they say?"

"Just that he was found dead in the woods."

"Are you safe?"

"Yeah."

"Where are you?"

"At the office."

"Who's with you?"

"Some of the volunteers."

"Stay away from the windows and don't let anyone take public transportation home. I will get private transportation to take everyone home."

"We good. We got rides."

When the tear-filled conversation ended, Yvonne texted Derrick. *"They murdered Quelle."*

He texted back from his bedroom. *"Where are you?"*

"n my room"

"I'll come down"

"No. I'm ok. I need u 2 get guards 4 my captains"

"On it"

"Thanks. Leaving n morning 4 w penn"

"I'm sending guard for you too."

Yvonne didn't text back. Wrapped in the long white silk robe over her cream and white-striped silk pajama pants, she ambled from the room and headed toward the spiral staircase. Motion lights lit her path as she dragged herself up the stairs with one hand on the banister. The thought of detouring to Derrick's bedroom entered her mind, but she headed to the solarium. When she entered, the bright lights replaced the darkness inside the room.

"Jacob, low volume Nina Simone favorites," she said, and four women came to mind. The tranquil sound of water sloshing and bouncing off the sandstone rocks that surrounded the pond of anubias plants added to the moment of serenity.

In her melancholy state, Yvonne sauntered along the circular granite path that divided the plants and trees. With her outstretched fingers lightly brushing the leaves on both sides, she was singing, "...I say, it's alright..." when lightning flashed across her eyes and she heard what sounded like a mangled voice in the roar of thunder.

She froze, wondering if the sound was her imagination. Her head tilted up at the glass ceiling. She was staring at the dark sky when the rain suddenly blocked the view and drowned out the music.

Yvonne lowered her head and stared at the eight-foot fern tree. Her heavy-hearted thoughts were interrupted by the mist that sprayed the one-minute warning before the solarium hosing, but she didn't leave the room. She turned again toward the rain that had blocked the sky. *Are these the tears from the souls in heaven for the innocent slain on earth?* She cried in that thought, and the hosing followed.

Soaked, Yvonne stood as if she was a part of the downpour outside the glass windows. "Quelle, I can see your spirit in the rain," she said with the understanding that death occurs in an instant, but the life taken renews at that moment. In her spiritual thoughts, she veered to the tree that Derrick named the tree of life and prayed in silence.

The downpour ended as quickly as it had started, and "To be young, gifted and black" bellowed from the voice of Nina Simone.

In the morning, Yvonne was on one of the three Unity Corporation private jets. With mixed anger and anguish, she entered the campaign office in Allegheny County and grieved with the staff and volunteers.

After Yvonne spoke to the police, she sensed a cover-up and hired a private investigator. She also posted $50,000 for information that led to an arrest.

The media reported that Quelle was beaten to death for an unknown reason. XOF news reported the murder as a hate crime for his sexuality. But Yvonne believed the murder was to prevent Quelle from influencing the voters in western Pennsylvania as he had in Alabama. That premise became credible when the campaign offices in Allegheny, Armstrong, and Beaver counties were bombed in the middle of the night.

But the staff and volunteers weren't deterred. They made makeshift offices at the local diners where they ate breakfast, lunch, and dinner, and used their personal phones and laptops to call voters, search the internet, and post information on social media.

Local and national news outlets covered their actions, which added volunteers for the campaign against the reelection of President Donaldson. The media attention also brought an overflow of daily customers for the diners.

* * *

Derrick didn't show any outward emotion over the news of Quelle's death, but the mirror within reflected his grief. Minutes later, his concealed anguish became visible when he received the text about another shooting on one of his properties.

Emy, who was sitting on the bedroom sofa with her feet unable to touch the floor, spoke in Tagalog.

"Mama, speak English," Juna said.

"These bad people. Children of devil," Emy said.

With her eyes on Derrick, Juna said, "We always thought America was safe place."

"No place on this earth is safe," Derrick said. "Not even in your own home. All you can do is pray and take precautions. I thank God that no one was injured."

"Yes, thank God that he protects them," Emy said.

Derrick ran a hand down his face as if wiping invisible tears.

"I'm not afraid," Juna said.

"I'm not afraid," Emy said. "You will win because God with you."

Uplifted by their words, he said with pep in his voice. "Yes, we will, and yes, He is."

"I get scared sometimes," Juna said.

Derrick embraced her. "Me too. But don't be afraid. Don't fear them. I'm the one they want."

"They can't have you. I won't let them."

"That's the attitude. That's how we will win."

CHAPTER 15

The Deep State hosted its annual goddess of fertility celebration at Erich Hornsby's Virginia castle. Among the attendees were current and former presidents, current and former members of Congress, current and former attorneys general, retired and active generals, and esteemed businessmen in America and other parts of the world.

To keep their identities secret from the servants and others, the six hundred and sixty-six men in attendance wore separate masks that covered their entire faces. They were also forbidden to speak to prevent voice recognition.

Each wore a black medieval robe with pointed hood that covered their naked bodies except for Hornsby and the priest. They wore scarlet, silk-hooded robes. Hornsby had the Minotaur mask. The priest wore the Anubis mask. All of the men wore white gloves to prevent leaving fingerprints and revealing identifiable hands.

Dark liturgical music was playing in every space of the castle. Inside the Great Hall lighted by the thousand candles, which were a thousand points of light, Hornsby and the priest were sitting on matching solid gold thrones that had a pentagram engraved above their heads.

Encased in the black marble wall behind them were the bronze busts of Constantine the Great, Otto the Great, and Adolf Hitler. Off-white marble statues of every Roman/Greek god and goddess surrounded the six-hundred and sixty-four men that faced them. Gargoyles as pillars circled the high ceiling.

When the priest stood, the music stopped. He stepped to the gold lectern that had the pentagram etched in the middle. In an altered voice, he lifted his hands and said in Latin, "Hail Diana, mother of God."

He opened the Gutenberg Bible that was on the lectern and marked himself with the sign of death before he said in Latin, "He that dwelleth in the help of the Most High."

He lifted his arms and tilted his head upward. "Raise the Fourth Reich!" he said in Latin.

The six-hundred and sixty-four men parted like the red sea to open the path for the sixteen-year-old virgin that choreographically came forward as they spoke in tongues.

Clothed only in the see-through white robe, she kneeled in front of the priest. He placed his right hand on top of her head with his eyes directed at the men that faced him, and said in Latin, "At midnight, this virgin is given to he who wears the Minotaur mask. May a boy be conceived."

When Hornsby stood, everyone inside the room marked themselves with the sign of death.

He lifted his hands upward with open palms, and said, "Go, and make worship with the goddess of fertility!"

The music returned, and everyone departed from the Great Hall except Hornsby and the council members. The others went into the many designated rooms where orgies and sexcapades occurred with the twelve hundred international females that were high-priced hookers and porn actresses. They were fully naked and wore the half-masks of bunnies, colored-eggs, and lambs, so their mouths would be free for fellatio and cunnilingus.

Some of the females were under eighteen, and a few were age twelve. Added to them were forty that had tits and a penis. They also went about naked and wore lioness half-masks.

The preselected females for Hornsby and the council members waited on the red velvet sofas in the hallway outside the Great Hall.

In the meeting, Hornsby said, "Don't forget, the uneducated white voters are our base. If we continue promoting bigotry, they won't look to see or hear anything else. But the educated voters are the problem. We can't mislead them by denying and deflecting the things that expose us. That is why those in the suburbs have turned away."

"That's because of Donaldson," Hindenburg said. "He's sloppy and can't keep his mouth shut. The stupid bastard. Let's kill him while he's here."

"We can't kill him now. The bulk of our base will recede. He has become their inspiration, their last hope for the new confederacy. He's a useful idiot."

"So how are we going to win back the suburbs with him at the head of the ticket?"

"We can't. We have to win without the suburbs."

"How are we going to do that?"

"We will continue suppressing the black voters," Murt interjected. "Those niggers won't stay in line for seven hours."

Hornsby said, "Keep track of the voters. Those who vote against Donaldson are enemies of the Reich. Those who don't vote are enemies of the Reich. Collect their names and addresses, and we will deal with them later."

"What do we do with the Jews and niggers that vote for Donaldson?" Murt asked.

"We spare them for now. We might be able to use them for a purpose. If not, they will become a part of the genocide."

Applause erupted.

Hornsby stood. "Okay, gentlemen, let's celebrate Pascha. Meeting adjourned."

* * *

In Harlem, the streetlights came on as dusk settled across the spring sky. The hotel's revolving door spun like waves in the ocean. Inside the adjacent restaurant, picture windows divided the patrons from the bustling sidewalk.

Derrick, Juna, and their children were inside the enclosed private booth. Two bodyguards stood outside the only entrance.

"I don't like living this way," Derrick said as he rubbed Malachi's head.

Juna opened her mouth but she said nothing.

Rhea-Toni was whimpering and woke Anthony.

Derrick lifted her out of the child seat and kissed her. She stopped crying, and he kissed her again. "You just want some attention from your daddy."

Juna smiled. "I'm jealous. She's closer to you than me."

He handed Rhea-Toni to her. "She has all the beauty of her mother."

Juna smacked her lips on her daughter's cheek and lifted her eyes to Derrick. "I love you."

He kissed her.

They finished their meal and headed for the exit with one bodyguard in front and the other behind. Derrick was holding the hand of Malachi, and Juna was pushing the double-seat stroller. Sideways glances that didn't go unnoticed followed their departure from the restaurant.

They entered the armored SUV. Juna sat on one side with Anthony on her lap and Derrick on the other with Rhea-Toni on his lap. Malachi sat quietly in the middle.

When the home elevator opened, Malachi brightened up and yelled in Tagalog, "Lola (Grandma)," and scooted into Emy's arms. Derrick carried Rhea-Toni to her bed, and Juna placed Anthony in his. Ten minutes later, Emy led Malachi by hand to the master bedroom and said, "Goodnight."

"Goodnight, Ma," Juna and Derrick replied.

Via the spiral staircase, Emy went back downstairs to her bedroom.

Preoccupied, Derrick stepped out onto the bedroom terrace. The tune by Regard & Frankie Wah soothed his thoughts with memories of his first sunset with Juna. He lowered his head and stretched his arms over the railing. The next tune, by Dusky, captured the moment as he stared at the metropolis.

As the minutes passed, the spirits of abused slaves cried within him. Retribution for slavery came to mind. As the 2018 tune by Young Nudy played the background, he gazed into the night, thinking about the many that had, and would, betray their brother for a dollar.

With his eyes locked on the brightest star, Derrick recited, "Blessed are they that do his commandments, that they may have right to the tree of life, and may enter in through the gates into the city. For without are dogs, and sorcerers, and whoremongers, and murderers, and idolaters, and whosoever loveth and maketh a lie." (Revelation 22:14-15)

His eyes dropped to the Manhattan skyline, and he ruminated on the calamitous events written in the book of Revelation and felt the hour was nigh as the 2019 Lonny X tune played the background.

He was nodding a lot to 21 Savage when Juna stepped onto the terrace and wrapped her arms around him from the back. Her head lay sideways on his left shoulder. Derrick turned, and they kissed.

"Jacob, play Gagong Rapper," Juna said.

Intimate touches and passionate kisses led to lovemaking under the starry night.

* * *

Dressed in the gold, untucked Kobe Bryant jersey, loose blue jeans, and white sneakers, Derrick was walking in Central Park without a bodyguard. Joggers and some with strollers passed by without recognizing him.

Familiar steps led him to Bow Bridge. In spiritual consciousness, he leaned over the stone railing to watch the rowboats afloat in both directions. Memories with Juna in one of those boats came to mind.

He continued across the pedestrian walkway and sat on the old wooden bench at the edge of the lake. He peered across with his thoughts on Mister, Junior, and others that were taken away by gun violence.

After a few minutes in that lugubrious state, he followed the path toward his home. Along the way, a middle-aged black man, who appeared to be destitute, was preaching at the edge of the paved path. Derrick stopped to listen.

The man, with yellowish eyes and stained teeth, greeted Derrick, "Praise be the Lord, my friend! Do you believe in the word of God?"

"Yes."

"Hallelujah!"

Derrick grinned at the man's joy for God.

"My friend, beware of rich men! Their greed and selfishness are the cause of many deaths." He turned the pages of his Bible and read, "'And Jesus looked round about, and saith unto his disciples, How hardly shall they that have riches enter into the kingdom of God! And the disciples were astonished at his words. But Jesus answereth again, and saith unto them, Children, how hard is it for them that trust in riches to enter into the kingdom of God! It is easier for a camel to go through the eye of a needle, than for a rich man to enter into the kingdom of God.'" (St. Mark 10:23-25)

The man lifted his eyes to Derrick and smiled. "If any man uses the words of a prophet or apostle to contradict those Scriptures that came from the mouth of Jesus Christ himself, that man is a deceitful spirit."

Derrick stared intently. "I agree with that. But the Scriptures recited are out of context and not complete."

The man's demeanor changed. He replied, irritated, "You only believe the Scriptures you like. Nothing I said is out of context or incomplete. You are confused because you read from another version of the Holy Bible."

"I read from the same Bible in your hand, the Authorized King James Version."

"Then you are like those who see but cannot perceive, and hear but cannot understand."

"Maybe those words you just spoke are meant for you to hear. It's written in the Scriptures that you read, 'how hard is it for them that trust in riches to enter into the kingdom of God!' It's hard for them that TRUST in riches. That is the context. If you continue reading, the next Scriptures say, 'And they were astonished out of measure, saying among themselves, Who then can be saved? And Jesus looking upon them saith, With men it is impossible, but not with God; for with God all things are possible.'"

The man's expression said he didn't understand the words.

"Those who put their trust in riches are without God," Derrick said. "But those who are rich and do not put their trust in riches are with God by faith, and their works include feeding the hungry and clothing the naked. That is the full understanding of the Scriptures you recited. Don't condemn a man because he's rich. A rich man is judged by what he does with his wealth."

Derrick pulled out his phone and scrolled the Scriptures folder. "It's written in III John 1:2 'Beloved, I wish above all things that thou mayest prosper and be in health, even as thy soul prospereth.' You see, we should prosper even as our soul prospers. A man is made rich to help the poor. But many are seduced by greed and selfishness to turn their back on the poor.

"You are correct that the word from Jesus Himself is greater than all. But the Bible tells us that we should live by every word of God. So there is relevance in every word of the Bible. We cannot take the New Testament and ignore the Old, neither the Old and ignore the New.

"It's written, '...every man should eat and drink, and enjoy the good of all his labour, it is the gift of God.'"

"Where is that Scripture found?" the man asked.

"Ecclesiastes 3:13."

The man turned the pages of his Bible to that Scripture and read silently. He humbly nodded after.

Derrick shook his hand and departed.

A venture that began in the late morning ended in the early evening.

* * *

As the spring settled into summer, vandalism in the Unity Corporation communities continued to mount across the country. No additional lives were lost, neither were there any injuries, but the fires and bombings resulted in the black-owned insurance companies joining other insurers to deny coverage for businesses in the black economic empowerment communities. The crisis prompted an in-person meeting with the Unity Corporation heads.

Shareese greeted Xavier and Gladys at the corporation headquarters in Upper Manhattan and escorted them into Derrick's office.

"Can I get you something to drink?" she asked.

"No, thank you," they both replied.

She shifted her smile to Derrick. "Do you need anything?"

"No, we're good. Thanks, Shareese," he replied as he stood with Yvonne at his side.

Shareese turned and left the room.

"Is that the same woman that attended your wedding?" Gladys asked Derrick.

"That's her. You saw her after hours."

"She's very impressive during and after hours."

The four giggled and sat on the chrome-handled tan leather chairs at the round, eight-person walnut table in the middle of the spacious and opulently furnished office.

"Without insurance," Derrick said, "we will become bankrupt if the attacks continue. Our only option is to capture the culprits."

"We can't trust the police," Xavier said. "They got videos of the perpetrators in action. Their faces are covered, but you can see they are white teens and young adults. I'm sure there are some good leads in the videos that they can use to find them."

"I agree," Derrick said. "We have to take matters into our own hands."

Yvonne interjected, "Derrick, are you suggesting violence?"

"No. I'm suggesting offering a reward."

"I offered $50,000 for information on Quelle's murder but got nothing. The private investigator connected the dots to the sheriff's son. But no one is willing to testify in court. How much are you suggesting?"

Derrick looked at them and said, "$100,000 for an arrest, and another $50,000 if convicted."

"Why don't you just make it $150,000 for arrest and conviction?" Yvonne said.

Xavier and Gladys joined the wait for his response.

He leaned forward with his hands clasped on the shiny table. "This is what I'm thinking." He shifted his eyes to his mother. "Mr. Hornsby told you about this kind. Now they are counting pennies instead of dimes, and we are the reason. They are the ones who hired those teens and young adults to vandalize our property. They aren't trying to kill but want to run us out of business.

"The mistake they made was hiring teens because they like to talk and brag to their friends. I'm betting that they are not among the privileged but considered by whitey, as 'poor white trash,' who will do anything for a buck.

"In almost every video of the crimes, the culprits are teens. Those teens have told their friends what they did and probably showed the money they got, which is probably no more than a couple of hundred dollars. By offering $100,000 for information that leads to an arrest for the vandalism, and $50,000 extra if convicted, I believe it will provide the incentive for the snitch to offer information that will not only arrest the person but convict them. I believe that separating the reward gives more incentive. Like when the price of an item is $4.99, some see four dollars and not five."

Xavier said, "At the amount you are suggesting, we have to allocate three million dollars to cover the reward for every attack. Why don't we just open our own insurance company?"

"We will. But that doesn't stop the attacks. Arrests will stop the attacks."

"What good will that do if they tell the police and the police bury the information because they know the perpetrators, or because they're racist cops?"

"I propose that we have the information come directly to the hotline that we monitor, and then forward the credible information to the media and FBI."

"How will you determine the credible tips?" Yvonne asked. "You know you're gonna get a bunch of callers with guesses. That's what happened on the Quelle tip line."

"There is information that only we and the police know. We can program the hotline to ask specific questions. If the tipper answers correctly, that is a credible tip."

They nodded.

Derrick added, "The media and FBI are weapons we need to use. Hornsby controls the head of the justice department but not the media. That's why he is always railing against the media and calling them the enemy of the people, because they tell the facts, and not alternative facts. If we send credible information to the media, they will broadcast it. The FBI is investigating because they have categorized the vandalism as hate crimes, despite opposition from the attorney general. The head of the FBI has proven to be loyal to the rule of law and not Donaldson or Hornsby, so he is an asset for us. We need to feed the FBI and the media all credible information. If the justice department curtails the FBI investigation, they won't be able to stop the media."

The meeting continued for another two hours on other pertinent matters. When Xavier and Gladys departed, Derrick locked eyes on his mother.

"Ma, Quelle was murdered because he was peeling voters away from Donaldson, and you are planning to finish the work he started. Quelle didn't know they were going to kill him. You know they killed him and will kill you too because you are trying to finish his work. Where is the wisdom in that?"

"Can I speak now?"

"No," Derrick angrily said. "You are the one that quoted the Scripture where Jesus walked in Galilee but not in Jewry because the Jews sought to kill him. So, why are you walking into the same county where Quelle was murdered?"

"Because I have no fear."

"It's not about fear. It's about being wise. Jesus didn't show fear when he didn't openly walk into places where people sought to kill him; he showed wisdom. Where has your wisdom gone?"

Yvonne leaned forward, elbows on the table, staring at him. "Wisdom is strategic. When the person or persons who murdered Quelle see a black woman walking in his footsteps without bodyguards, they will know that I don't fear them and wonder why.

"You mentioned the media is one of the weapons that we have to use. I'm ahead of you. I have a reporter who will interview me while I'm in the county and follow me on the first day of knocking on doors. The word will get out, and people who don't watch the Peacock will watch to hear what I am saying about their rural counties, and why I'm not afraid.

"That's what I want and what we need. If I can get them to listen, I can open some eyes. That's how Quelle helped us win in Alabama, and that's what he was doing in Pennsylvania. Political power controls this country. If I have to lay down my life, let it be in the fight for political power that protects my children and grandchildren."

"Are you going to carry your gun with you?"

"I won't because I will have to get a concealed carry permit. If I do, my enemies in the counties will know, and the corrupt sheriff will arrest me on some trumped-up charges, like I threatened someone when I knocked on the door. They might even kill me by saying that I pointed my gun at one of the people whose door I knocked on. I'm not going to fall into that trap, and I'm not going to carry a concealed gun without a permit because I know I will be stopped and checked. My faith is my rod. The Holy Ghost is my staff."

Derrick stared with a wrinkled forehead.

* * *

The next day, Derrick held a press conference in front of one of the bombed stores in Washington, DC.

He pointed to the charred buildings behind him. "This is what hate looks like. We are offering a $100,000 reward for information that leads to an arrest for the damages done to any of our economic empowerment communities, and an extra $50,000 if the person or persons are convicted."

He could feel that statement made the impact intended and paused before he said, "I will now take questions."

He pointed to the black lady that had her hand raised at the back.

"Mr. Williams, is it true the businesses in your communities are no longer insured? And what do you think about the black-owned insurance companies who turned their back to you?"

"The Unity Corporation has recently formed its own insurance company, so all businesses in our communities are insured. As for the insurers who decided not to continue our partnership, we are disappointed, but it isn't a setback."

He pointed to another raised hand at the back.

"Are you positioning yourself to start a revolution?"

"If the revolution is political, because we need another political revolution. The first one occurred when the black president was elected. That was a political revolution that galvanized young and old voters, black and white voters, blue and white collar, the inner cities and the suburbs. His inspirational voice was able to bring out those who hadn't voted in decades.

"We need a revolution to remove the revolution that elected Donaldson. We also need to be aware of those on the Left who will not vote unless their candidate is the nominee. That feeble mindset contributed to Donaldson getting elected.

"Big picture: one percent of the people in this country control it. That one percent is buying the presidential and congressional elections to benefit them. If the one percent becomes two percent, the one percent has lost money. Because of their greed and selfishness, they will do everything in their power to prevent that from happening.

"Influential people on the left believe the voters in America are not ready for a political revolution. Again, that belief was proven false when a black man was elected president and then reelected. That was a political revolution that we as a people didn't maintain. We made a change but didn't build on it, and now we have a racist in the White House who is trying to remove the legacy of the two-term black president.

"I blame the establishment on the Left for rigging the system four years ago to nominate their preferred candidate, who was flawed and whose underhandedness became exposed to the American public.

"So now we have started a new political revolution by endorsing inspirational moderate and progressive candidates that appeal to both young and old, who put country before party."

He pointed to the raised hand in the front.

"Business Plus has predicted the Unity Corporation will bankrupt in six months. What do you have to say about that?"

"Those who choose to believe it, let them."

He pointed to the raised hand in the middle.

"The Unity Corporation didn't endorse any of the black candidates during the primary. Why?"

"We didn't endorse any of the black candidates in the primary because we didn't believe any of them could win the general election in this political climate. So, we waited to see who would win the nomination, and the person we expected won.

"We see ourselves as independents. We lean to the Left but will vote on the Right if the Left is wrong in our view. We put country before party. Unlike the party of President Donaldson, we will not defend any manner of corruption or lies because the politician is popular.

"We believe a prominent white male with a black woman as VP will win the states needed to prevent John Donaldson from having another electoral college victory. I encourage all to get out and vote, especially the young, because the political revolution cannot occur without the young."

* * *

The weekly vandalism on the Unity Corporation properties stopped after tips led to arrests in nineteen of the twenty-three attacks. Three weeks had passed without any additional vandalism.

The insurance risks seemingly lessened. The black-owned companies wanted to reinstate their coverage, but Derrick didn't renew the partnership. He had expanded the Unity Corporation's newly formed insurance company to include home and auto, and in less than thirty days, his insurance company had 18 percent of the market share.

With the dollar circulating many times over in the black economic empowerment communities, black unemployment dropped significantly and salaries increased. The minimum wage at the Unity Corporation businesses was $19 per hour.

In fame and shared fortune, Derrick was in the comfort of his home with his wife and kids in the designated family area. The tune by Gil Scot Heron & Makaya McCraven played in the background. "I remember when I was new here," Juna said.

He kissed her. "I will always take care of you."

CHAPTER 16

On the day after Charlene's wedding, Yvonne flew to western Pennsylvania to follow the road map written by Quelle, whose murder remained unsolved.

On her second day in Allegheny County, Yvonne continued to knock on the doors of homes that had John Donaldson's signs and Confederate flags as warning notices. Some ignored her knocks, others shouted vulgarity behind their closed doors, but one answered.

A thin and ungroomed fifty-something man opened the door with anger in his eyes and a can of beer in his hairy hand. "Get the fuck off of my property," he yelled from behind the frayed screen.

Yvonne smiled and humbly said, "Thank you, sir, for opening your door."

As if his body was rejecting the thoughts at the forefront of his mind, his face turned into a blank expression.

Yvonne kindly said, "Sir, are you angry at me because I'm black?"

"No!" he shouted. "I'm tired of people trying to tell me who I should vote for."

"Sir, who are you voting for?"

"None of your damn business!"

Yvonne maintained her smile. "Sir, I would like to know. Your home is the only one on this stretch without a John Donaldson sign."

"I don't need no damn sign. I might vote for him, and I might not. Hell, I might not vote at all."

"Sir, have you considered voting for his opponent?"

He shook his head and frowned. "No!"

"Why not? I'd like to know. Maybe I'm voting for the wrong person."

"You damned liberals are always voting for the wrong things." He sniffed and tilted the beer to his mouth.

"It's hot, and that beer looks cold. Can I have one?"

His eyes narrowed, and he scratched the stubble.

"I really would like to have a beer."

He appeared undecided.

"I'll buy it from you."

"You want to come in, or you want me to bring it to you?"

"I'd like to come in if you don't mind. I've been on my feet for hours. It would be nice to sit down and drink a cold beer."

"C'mon on in." He opened the screen door and pointed. "Have a seat over there."

She sat on the yellow floral chair with her feet on the thin, burgundy-carpeted floor. The trailer home was filled with the stench from cigarette smoke.

The man scratched his scruff with dirt-filled nails. "You don't smoke do you?"

"No, I don't. How did you know?"

"Your face. Sorry 'bout the smell. My wife smokes a lot."

"Oh, where is she? I want to meet her."

"She's at work," he grumbled and walked toward the aged refrigerator. His khakis were wet, as if he forgot to use the bathroom. His dingy, white, half T-shirt didn't cover the edge of his dingy briefs.

Yvonne was discreetly scanning the surroundings when he returned with the beer. "Thank you, sir. How much?"

"Go ahead and drink it. It's free." He sat on the matching sofa.

She popped the top and sipped. "Sir, can I know your name?"

"George. Yours?"

"Yvonne."

"You look familiar. Where have I seen you?"

"Maybe on television. I've been on a few news talk shows."

He gulped his beer. "I'm sure I didn't see you there. I don't watch liberal news."

"You probably saw me on XOF."

"You were on XOF?"

"I was. Do you watch the show with the black woman host?"

"I do. Sooo, th-that's where I saw you?"

"Maybe."

He stared with a touch of anger in his eyes. "You don't drink beer."

"Let me be honest with you. I don't like beer. I only asked because I wanted the chance to speak with you."

"Uh-huh. So, what do you want to talk about? The election?"

"I do. I need you to help me understand why this county supports the president?"

He drank the remainder of his beer and belched. "Because he's doing a good job."

"But he's a liar, and has abused his power, and obstructed justice."

"All politicians are liars. You lied to get invited in here."

"I did, and I confessed. I apologized and told you the reason why I lied. But Donaldson doubles and triples down on his lies. He tries to make you believe that two plus two isn't four."

"That sounds like some liberal talking point to take my eyes off the big picture."

"And what's the big picture?"

"The wall."

"Why is the wall important to you?"

"We need to protect our borders. If you don't have borders, you don't have a country. All immigrants need to enter this country legally."

"I agree. But the wall isn't the solution because the majority of illegal immigrants are those who enter through airports and overstay their visas."

"That's more liberal talking points."

Yvonne scooted forward and sat the beer on the worn coffee table in front of him. "George, is your life better than it was four years ago."

"Better how?"

"Better at the kitchen table."

He pondered the question.

She waited patiently for his answer.

"Now that I think about it, I have less than I had four years ago."

"Do you mean money?"

"Yes."

"So, why are you supporting the president?"

"He's doing a good job. He cut taxes. The country has record unemployment and a record stock market."

"Did you benefit from the tax cut?"

"We got a little something."

"If you don't mind, how much?"

"That's none of your business."

"You're right, it's not. But I'm guessing only a hundred at the most. While you were happy receiving that little something, you didn't notice that food went up, and prescription costs, and your electric and water bills. George, I bet if you count the amount you received from the tax cut and subtract the increase in your monthly expenses, you will discover that when money went into one pocket, a hand was taking much more from your other pocket. You paid for the rich to benefit from the tax cut."

"That's okay, because the rich can provide more jobs if they have more money."

"Have they?"

"I don't know. Probably. We have record low unemployment. Somebody is hiring."

"Are you employed?"

"No."

"How long have you been unemployed?"

"Two years."

"If you don't mind answering, why are you unemployed?"

"The factory closed."

"The president said he was bringing back factory jobs. So that's another of his many false promises."

George's expression seemed to disagree with that statement, but he didn't respond.

"Do you own stock?" she asked.

"No."

"So, the low unemployment isn't benefiting you because you are unemployed, and the record stock market isn't benefitting you because you don't own stock."

"It's not harming me either."

"Yes, it is. The unemployment numbers are low because the president removed the regulations that were put in place to combat climate change. Global warming is real. I'm sure you heard about the ice melting in Antarctica. That's the fifth-largest continent, larger than Europe and Australia. What do you think will happen if Antarctica melts? Where will all that water go?"

His eyes bulged as if he realized the possibility.

"George, based on your answers, there is nothing in the president's policies that benefit you except the wall. If the wall is more important than what's on your kitchen table, you should vote to reelect the president. But if not, you need to vote for the person that will improve your personal life. Voting is personal. Vote for the candidate that is helping you personally. This county was better off under the black president, but voted against his reelection. Why?"

He didn't answer.

Yvonne kept her focus on his lowered half-bald head.

He lifted his head. "I voted for the men who ran against him."

"Let me say that those men are very good. If I lived in Arizona, I would've voted for him to be in the Senate. If I lived in Utah, I would've voted for him to be in the Senate."

"So why didn't you vote for them when they ran for president?"

"Because I believed the black president was better."

"I think you voted for him because he was black."

"It was one of the reasons, but not the main reason."

"What was the main reason?"

"His policies."

"Liberalism?"

"No. Healthcare mainly. Why didn't you vote for him when he ran for reelection? You said your life was better during that time."

"Because I'm a Republican. I always vote republican like you always vote democrat."

"I'm a registered Democrat, but I don't always vote democrat. I believe in what's written on this T-shirt: country before party. You should put country before party and vote for the person that will make your life and the life of your children better. If that's the current president, then vote for him. But if it isn't, choose country over party."

Yvonne stood. "Thank you for the beer. I appreciate the time you gave me and the conversation we shared." She could see in his eyes that he was considering her words. "Goodbye, George, and thanks again." She turned and headed for the open door.

George followed, but she didn't look back at him. She hoped she had gotten through to him.

* * *

The leaves on the deciduous trees had turned yellow; sweaters had replaced the sleeveless shirts; shorter days and longer nights had filled the sky.

Yvonne lay asleep in Terrance's bed. Awakened by the unknown, she was surprised that Terrance wasn't next to her. She sat up with the covers clutched above her breasts, and her naked back pressed against the gray microfiber headboard, looking around for him.

The bathroom door was open, but the lights were off. The bedroom door wasn't open. *He must be downstairs.*

The morning light was gleaming through the open blinds as she leaned across the king-sized bed and lifted the remote from the bedside table. She turned on the television, lowered the volume, and flicked the channels to AM Joy.

Moments later, she heard footsteps coming up the stairs with the smell of bacon and omelets. She smiled with her eyes on the bedroom door.

Her smile widened when Terrance entered with a white wicker breakfast tray.

"Good morning." He set the four-legged tray on the terracotta-colored comforter over her lap.

"Thank you," she said, and their lips touched. "Where's your breakfast?"

Without a reply, he scooted down the steps in his checkered boxers and quickly returned with a silver breakfast tray.

He set the tray behind Yvonne's and climbed under the covers next to her, then placed the silver tray over his lap. They chatted while they were eating. When the bacon and omelets were gone, Terrance removed a small dark pouch from the bottom bowl of his strawberries. He looked into her eyes, opened the pouch, and lifted out the ring. "Will you marry me?"

Yvonne smiled with tears.

Terrance broadened his smile as if her tears were those of joy.

She cupped her hands with unsure eyes. Her head lowered, and her hands tightened.

His smile quickly faded.

Her fingers wiped the rolling tears. "I love you, Terrance, but I can't marry you right now."

"Why?"

She held his hands and locked eyes with him. "The election is next month."

"What does the election have to do with you saying yes or no?"

She squeezed his hands, lowered her head, and slowly shook.

"What's wrong, Yvonne?"

She lifted her head. "After the election, I have to go away until the inauguration. But if Donaldson wins, I'm not sure how long I will be gone."

"What are you talking about?"

"I'm talking about what I've been telling you for the past six months. Have you stored food and water?"

"I told you that I'm in the fight with you. I know what time it is. In the school's basement, we have enough food and water to nourish two hundred people for three and a half years. All of your son's schools serve as a refuge. But I don't understand why you have to leave?"

"Precaution."

"Precaution? I'm your safety net."

She blinked slowly. "Terrance, if Donaldson gets reelected, Erich Hornsby will kill him and become president. If Donaldson loses the election, Erich Hornsby might start the coup. If that happens, he will come after my son and me. That includes everyone close to me. I'm sure he knows about us. If it becomes known that we are engaged, he will come after you. I was planning to make this weekend our last."

"Our last?"

"Hear me out. I love you. I want to marry you. But I have to make it appear that our relationship is over. That way, they won't come after you in their search for me. Do you understand?"

"I understand, but I don't agree. I don't care if they come after me. I'm not afraid."

Her head dropped. She squeezed his hands then looked up. "Terrance, I need you to put your emotions to the side and use your wisdom. If they come for you, they will come for your children and their children. These are not animals; they are wild beasts without a compassionate cell in their bodies. They torture and kill without mercy for the child. We cannot match their earthly power, so we have to be smarter to avoid them. I need you to make them believe that we are no longer a couple."

"How am I supposed to do that?"

"Tell everyone that you proposed, and I said no. That will spread like must-hear gossip, and that's what we want, because they have ears around the people we know."

"Maybe they are listening to us right now."

"They are listening to our phone calls. That's why you have to call your children and close friends. Tell them that you proposed, and I didn't accept."

"Why do I have to say that I proposed and you didn't accept? Why not just say we broke up?"

"Because I'm sure you paid for that ring with your credit card, so they know you bought it." She chuckled. "Be Denzel for a minute and win an Oscar."

He chuckled.

"I love you," she said and kissed his palms. She clutched her fingers with his. "When Erich Hornsby is no longer the threat, I will return and happily marry you."

They kissed and made love before and after church.

CHAPTER 17

On the eve of the election, Yvonne was staring out her bedroom curtainless windows. Twenty-four days had passed since she had seen or talked to Terrance in the flesh. But in the spirit, she had spoken to him every day, feeling his thoughts as if her own.

Even at that moment looking out at the darkness surrounding the leafless trees, she saw his face, his eyes as the lights in the distance, his voice in her head, his hands as her hands.

Her carnal feelings mingling with the spiritual, Yvonne lay sideways under the bed covers, eyes wide-open in her darkened room. "Terrance, I can feel you. I know you can feel me," she whispered. "I am with you in the spirit, which is more real than the flesh. I love you."

* * *

On election night, Rhea-Toni and Anthony were asleep in their playpens, and Malachi slept in Emy's arms. Juna sat next to her on the sofa, with Derrick, Yvonne, Charlene, Amari, Gladys, and Xavier around them, all watching the 84-inch television. Blue, Shareese, Michael, and Judy had joined on the private portal.

The early results projected the Left as retaining control of Congress, but the presidential race was too close to call and entered the eleven o'clock hour.

"We are going to win Pennsylvania, Michigan, and Wisconsin," Derrick told the group.

"How come you sound so confident?" Judy asked.

"Four years ago, Donaldson won those rural counties by an average of ten thousand votes. But this year he is only winning by a little over two thousand. Based on the reporting, the turnout is larger than four years ago. When the major cities and suburbs in those states report their numbers, we will have a new president-elect. Ma, you and Quelle did it."

"Don't count your chickens before they hatch," Yvonne cautioned him.

Several minutes later, CBNSM, announced Matthew Miller as the president-elect.

After the celebratory hollers, hugs, and high-fives all around, Yvonne screamed, "We did it!"

"Yvonne, *you* did it," Gladys said.

Derrick interjected. "Yes, ma, you did it. We won the war for political power because of you."

Charlene wrapped her arms around her mother, who was crying. "What's wrong, Ma?"

Everyone looked at them. Derrick knew. *She's thinking about Terrance and Quelle.*

"M-Ma, what's wrong?" Charlene repeated.

Yvonne wiped her eyes. "I'm thinking about Terrance and Quelle."

Blue, Shareese, Michael, and Judy had questioning expressions because they didn't know about Terrance.

"Ma, Quelle is proud of you," Derrick said. "You kept his spirit on the earth. You finished what he started. I was wrong."

She nodded with her head lowered, then raised her head and said, "I'm sorry for spoiling the party."

"Ma, you haven't spoiled the party," Charlene said. "You're the reason for the celebration. We feel your pain. Remember, there is a positive side to every negative thing."

Yvonne smiled. "Thank you. I'm going to bed now." She stood and ambled down the spiral staircase.

Derrick turned to the television. "I want to hear Donaldson concede."

All eyes and ears were waiting for the same, but forty-one minutes later, he tweeted, "It's not over. The election was rigged. Stay tuned!"

"You said he wouldn't concede if he lost," Juna said to Derrick.

"It's time," he replied, looking at everyone.

* * *

At 9:10 a.m., the morning after the election, inside the White House briefing room, Hornsby was at the podium.

"The president isn't conceding because we do not believe we lost the election. We believe the Left rigged the system to allow their supporters to vote more than once. The president has ordered a nationwide recount. A commission led by Murt Pointer will oversee the process."

When he opened the floor to questions, one of the reporters said, "It's not lawful for the president to form a commission to oversee the recount. Under what authority can he proceed in that way?"

Hornsby grimaced. "The authority of the President of the United States of America."

Another reporter asked, "Throughout our history, there has always been a peaceful transition. Is the president concerned that his actions might lead to a civil war?"

"The president is concerned about the corruption from the Left!" Hornsby said. "The deep state is trying to steal the election. It's a coup before the eyes of the American people, an act of treason. We will stop the perpetrators by force."

He ignored the questions spurred by that comment and headed for the exit as reporters continued to shout for clarification.

The next day, the president read a prepared statement to the nation from the Oval Office.

"My fellow Americans, I will not concede the election. Our exit polls show that I was the clear winner. We have strong evidence that the Left rigged the system to allow unregistered people to vote. I have appointed a commission headed by Murt Pointer to investigate every vote, especially the mail-in ballots.

"The attorney general is investigating the Speaker of the House and the left-wing media on collaborating to rig the election. Until further notice, only XOF will have access to the White House.

"The Justice Department has issued an arrest for Minister Kabir. We discovered that he was harboring radical Islamic extremists who were planning major terrorist attacks in New York City and Washington, D.C.

"I took an oath to defend this country against foreign and domestic enemies. Russia is not the enemy. The leadership on the Left is the enemy.

"Believe me. I know more than our intelligence agencies and the generals. Our country is under attack by domestic enemies led by the Speaker of the House and the fake news media. It's treasonous, and I will bring everyone involved to justice. Believe me."

* * *

The president continued in the footsteps of Jefferson Davis and refused to comply with the directives from Congress and all federal court orders. The public was divided and confused by the irregular orders in the White House that continued when Hornsby ordered Donaldson to pardon ninety-two white supremacist men convicted of mass murder, rape, robbery, and war crimes, even the criminally insane.

The public and members of Congress on both sides of the aisle were openly outraged by the pardons. And without a permit, hundreds of thousands marched down Pennsylvania Avenue to the gates of the White House. Many of them set up tents and lit bonfires at night, burning red hats and Donaldson reelection paraphernalia.

But the president justified his actions with lies that his base believed and allies in Congress defended. XOF news continued to report the debunked conspiracy theory of voter fraud as the truth.

Six weeks before the scheduled presidential inauguration, Hornsby met privately with Donaldson in the Oval Office.

"Have you sent your family to Florida?" Hornsby asked.

From his seat behind the desk, Donaldson replied, "Yes. They left last night."

"Good. Keep your family there until this is over."

"I want it over now. The protesters are getting all the news, even on XOF. I'm declaring a state of emergency! I want those protesters removed from the gates!"

"In due time, all resistance will be crushed. Are you ready to take your place as president until you die?"

Donaldson had become emboldened by the outward support received from the base and loyalists in Congress. He barked at Hornsby, "I'm already president forever. I have the generals and the party under my command. I don't need you anymore."

Hornsby grinned. "Ah, is that so?"

Donaldson looked him directly in the eye and pointed, "You're fired! I don't need a vice-president."

Hornsby's grin extended, and he chuckled. He stood and leaned forward, palms on the desk. "What did you say?"

Donaldson defiantly replied, "You heard me. You're fired. I'm the one the people love. They want *me* to lead them, not you."

"This is how you treat the man who saved your ass in the Senate?"

"You didn't respect me before I became president, or after. Your mistake was saving my ass in the Senate. Now the party is unified under me. I don't need you."

Hornsby turned and called the agent that was standing outside the Oval Office door.

Donaldson's brows lifted. *Why is he calling him?*

Agent Garcia entered as if it was his first day on a new job. "Yes, sir?"

"Are you enjoying your new assignment?" Hornsby asked.

"Yes, sir. I'm grateful to be assigned to protect the president."

"Are you prepared to take a bullet for him?"

"Yes, sir! It's my duty."

"Who did you vote for?"

"Sir, I cannot divulge that information. It's against policy to discuss political issues. My job is to protect the president, regardless of party affiliation."

Hornsby walked past him and stood beside the confused president.

"Agent Garcia, I know who you, and everyone, voted for. You voted for Mitchell. You are from the deep state, sent to assassinate the president."

The agent had a befuddled expression. "What?"

Hornsby quickly pulled out his concealed gun and shot the agent.

In shock, Donaldson peed on himself, trembling, and begging for his life.

***

The gunshot was heard throughout the West Wing, but all who were present in the White House were loyalists to the Fourth Reich and knew the meaning.

On the White House lawn was a bevy of reporters from around the world. They heard the gunshot and scrambled to learn the reason, but were prevented by the SS from entering.

As if he couldn't hear Donaldson whining, Hornsby calmly walked over to the dead body and removed the agent's gun.

He turned, gun in hand, and frowned at Donaldson's fearful expression. "Relax, I saved your life. The deep state sent him to assassinate you."

Breathing heavily, Donaldson said, "Th-thank you. I'm not firing you. I need you. Forgive me."

Hornsby shifted his eyes to the door. As if on cue, another agent entered the Oval Office with his gun drawn and stood over the dead body.

Relieved, Donaldson stood and said to the familiar face, "That man was sent to kill me!"

"No, I'm the one sent to kill you," the agent said. The only times the president wasn't wearing the bulletproof vest were in the shower and tanning booth, so he shot him in the head.

The reporters heard the second shot, and chaos ensued with speculation broadcast live.

A few minutes later, the press secretary stepped out onto the White House lawn and faced the reporters. "The president was shot and killed by agent Alejandro Garcia, who was recently assigned to protect the president. Agent Daniel Winston responded and killed the assassin. We suspect that agent Garcia was a member of the deep state. That is all I can tell you at this time. Please pray for our country."

She turned and headed for the White House door as the reporters shouted questions.

Cleaners assigned to rearrange the murder scene entered the Oval Office and completed their work without disturbance.

* * *

The world was reeling from the news of the president's assassination when subway bombings occurred in the District of Columbia, New York City, Los Angeles, and Chicago.

The media scrambled for details. The public, in fear and panic, were glued to their communication devices.

An hour later, inside the White House Situation Room, Hornsby sat at the head of the table with the six Joint Chiefs of Staff, the secretaries of defense and state, the attorney general, and the chief of staff. The broadcast was on every television channel and radio station.

"At 9:37 a.m., the president was assassinated in the Oval Office by newly assigned agent Alejandro Garcia. A swift investigation from the attorney general has linked the assassin to the deep state on the Left. We believe the president was getting too close to uncovering the corruption that stole the election. We have strong evidence that the Speaker of the House and the Senate majority leader, with help from the left-wing media, is attempting a coup. As your new president, I will do everything in my power to stop their treasonous actions. I have signed an executive order that temporarily suspends the powers of Congress and the freedom of the press.

"In another attempt to overthrow the government, there were synchronized bombings in several of our cities. The bombings were coordinated attacks from Islamic radicals who were allowed to enter our country because the previous administration didn't protect our borders. We will identify, arrest, and condemn the suspects.

"I am declaring a national state of emergency. Martial law goes into effect today at 6:00 p.m. Eastern Standard Time. I am imposing a twenty-four-hour curfew until further notice. Any unauthorized persons found on the streets after 6:00 p.m. will be arrested or shot.

"I am calling on all Americans to help their country in this time of crisis. Interested men and women can register to join the militia. Visit any police station to register as a volunteer to protect our streets from lawlessness.

"Also, within the next few days, the department of the treasury will begin issuing a new currency. You will need that currency to buy and sell in this country. All sanctioned banks will trade your current dollar bills and coins for the new currency. This action is taking place to bring the terrorists from out of hiding.

"I have closed all borders, the country and the states. No one is allowed to enter or leave the country or any state without White House approval. I have federalized the National Guard to protect everything within four square miles of the White House and to patrol the downtown areas in the major cities. The police and the militia will protect neighborhoods from lawlessness.

"This crisis will surely pass, because we will not allow domestic or foreign enemies to defeat us. God bless America, and God bless the people of the United States."

The faces of many who watched and heard had worry and fear written on them.

In the following hours, fear and panic emptied the grocery and convenience store shelves. In some stores, people were killed for the last candy bar.

The restaurants and fast-food merchants were sold out and closed. Delinquents raided homes for the items in refrigerators, freezers, and kitchen cabinets.

The police water-cannon vehicles and the national guardsmen forced the protesters from the gates of the White House and outside the four square miles.

The following morning at 4:02 a.m., DHS agents sprung from a helicopter that landed on the roof of Derrick's penthouse. They bombed the entrance and entered with assault rifles. Another group had access via the elevator and entered with their guns drawn. A thorough search on both floors didn't find anyone present.

The lead agent radioed the team at the residence of Xavier and Gladys. "Nothing found."

"Nothing here," came the reply.

* * *

Chaos had cornered Capitol Hill as DHS agents arrested the Speaker of the House and the Senate majority leader. All Muslim citizens and nonwhite immigrants were arrested and sent to internment camps. The outspoken reporters, media heads, and citizens that Hornsby deemed as enemies of the people were also arrested and sent to separate internment camps.

Hornsby added the local militia to guard the four-square-mile area. Dressed as deer hunters with red hats, the men and women of the militia outnumbered the national guard by thirty-to-one. They confiscated every building within the four square miles of the White House to use as military outposts.

Sanctioned to purge were the other members of the militia across the country that were led by the ninety-two pardoned criminals. They targeted the Jews and blacks in prominent communities, sodomizing and killing at will.

Some of the unrestrained militia ventured into the poor districts to terrorize the blacks and Hispanics. Outnumbered by persons and firepower, they fought back with guerrilla warfare and chased the militia from their neighborhoods. But the militia continued to wreak terror on the weak and vulnerable as they rode on the streets with long guns in American-made pickup trucks, voicing their bigotry with bullhorns.

Armed drones with loudspeakers circled to protect monuments, state capitols, and state and country borders. On the ground protecting those areas were troops, state, and local police.

In the absence of law enforcement patrolling neighborhoods, vigilantes guarded their streets, but some of them turned to criminality, raping neighbors they had secretly desired and murdering others that they didn't like for various reasons.

The lawlessness that began in the White House had swarmed the streets of America. What many believed could only occur in a movie became real-life. Mayhem had penetrated every neighborhood. And when some correctional officers abandoned their posts, prisoners ran free.

Gunfire, sirens, and whirring helicopters were the sounds outside every home, day and night. Bodies lay in the streets like roadkill, some slain because they left their homes in search of food and baby supplies, some because of looting, others because of curiosity, and others because of hate.

CHAPTER 18

In the secret luxury bunker built to withstand a nuclear blast, Derrick and Juna were sitting on the sofa, their children and Emy were next to them. Yvonne, Charlene, Amari, Gladys, and Xavier were sitting on the matching modular sectional sofa that faced them.

Under the stimulated natural light, Juna reached for Anthony and said to Derrick, "How much longer we have to stay here?"

"Until it's over," Derrick said. "We have everything we need to live here for five years."

Yvonne interjected, "Juna, we have to continue praying. We can see the protests are increasing. Even those on the Right in Congress who supported the president have secretly joined the resistance."

"Ma, how do you know that?" Charlene asked.

"Know what?"

"That some of Hornsby's allies have joined the resistance."

"I've been receiving encrypted messages from one of them."

Charlene turned to Derrick. "I'm with Juna. Where do we go from here?"

"We stay put and wait it out. The resistance is growing, and people in powerful positions are having second thoughts. Political power is still in our hands because the majority of the people are resisting coercion. Relax and stay patient. We are in one of the safest places on earth."

"But are Grandma Ruth and Grandma Beverly safe? We haven't heard from them."

"You know they are safe in the North Carolina bunker."

"But we haven't communicated with them since we've been down here. Can you call them?" Charlene pleaded.

"You know I can't take that chance. Their communication lines aren't secure."

"What if someone who knows about their bunker betrayed them?"

"We would've heard about it. We got television and the internet. Stay positive."

Charlene swung her eyes to Amari. "This ain't a movie! I'm scared!"

Amari gripped her hands and peered into her eyes.

"Say something!" she hollered.

"Charlene, if we get careless and take unnecessary chances, we might get caught. If we get caught, we will die. They don't want us. They want your brother. But to get to him, they will come for us. That's why we are here, to protect him. Juna hasn't asked about her family in Hawaii because she knows they're safe in the bunker that Derrick built on the resort. You know your family is safe. But you're the one having a panic attack. That's the mindset that leads to making a costly mistake."

Amari turned to the others. "We all knew the plan before we got here. We can't change it until we have no other choice. But I have a question." He looked at Yvonne. "Did you tell Terrance about this place?"

"I didn't tell anyone!"

"I'm sorry if I offended you. I just wanted to ease my mind."

She didn't reply.

"All of us are scared in some form or fashion," Gladys said, "but we all knew that this day might come. That's why we planned for it. Stick to the plan."

Derrick eyed Charlene. "Stephanie, Diane, Phyllis, Ruben, Steve, Great-Grandma, and Grandma are all safe. But I didn't tell other family members about the bunkers because I didn't trust that they would keep it a secret. We are in a life-or-death situation. Blood is thicker than water, but the soul is thicker than blood. There is a bounty on my head. I believe some family members are looking to collect."

"Family members?" Charlene said.

"Yes, family members."

Tears ran down her cheeks. "Derrick, how can you be so heartless? I've never seen this side of you."

His eyes narrowed with disappointment. "Charlene, how many times have I told you that wisdom overshadows love?"

"But they are family, Derrick! They have kids!"

"You know that I warned every family member about this day and gave a year's supply of food and water for them and their children and money to purchase additional supplies. I did all of that two months before the election. Grandma Beverly wasn't told about the bunkers because she can't keep a secret. Steve and Ruben took her and Grandma Ruth to the location. I told our aunts about the bunkers in their cities because I trusted them to keep the secret."

"I know Grandma Ruth, Steve, and Ruben wouldn't tell. But what made you so confident that our aunts wouldn't tell someone?" she asked.

"I tested our aunts with a false secret that enticed them to tell you or my mother, if not both. When I didn't hear it back from you or Ma, I knew they could keep a secret."

"What did you tell them?" Yvonne asked.

"It's a secret."

Charlene wiped the tears from her face. "What about Blue and Michael? Where are they? Where are the people that work at your headquarters? Have you turned your back on them too?"

Derrick held a neutral expression. "Michael and Judy are in France; Blue and Shareese are in Africa. When Donaldson didn't concede, they knew what to do. My staff was given a year's supply of food and water for a family of four. I haven't turned my back on them. But I can't allow one of them to know my whereabouts because torture can break a loyal person.

"They are offering twenty-five million dollars for my capture. Can you believe that? That's the same for Bin Laden. They are offering the same for Minister Kabir—two black men who are not terrorists or committed a crime. I can understand their fear of Minister Kabir because he had the power to gather a million black men into one place. While they were there for harmony and pride, the powers that be saw an army, they saw a million soldiers with guns. So, they want him dead. But they won't find him because he is in one of our Chicago bunkers.

He's been there for over a year. But why me? Why is my capture worth twenty-five million dollars?"

He leaned forward with his eyes locked on Charlene. "Because in their eyes, the black man who doesn't fear them is the most dangerous in the world."

Charlene turned to Amari and shrieked, "Is this the end of the world?"

"Only God knows the end," Amari said, "Relax. We are safe, and those who are not in bunkers are safe if they trust the Lord."

"Why didn't you warn other people? There are a lot of good people out there who didn't have a clue about what would happen? You only thought about the people in your church."

"Charlene," Amari said, "I'm seeing a woman in you that I don't love and cannot like."

"You don't love me now?" she wailed.

Derrick stared at her, and it was clear the others were surprised by her reaction.

Amari embraced her. "I love you, Charlene, but not the woman that you are allowing yourself to be right now."

"W-What y-you mean?"

"You just accused me of not caring for others. That's the same as calling me a hypocrite."

"I'm sorry."

"Are you really? You can't be sincere in your apology unless you understand why you were wrong. Do you?"

She lowered her head. "I know you're not a hypocrite."

"Look at me. Do you believe I only care about the people in my church?"

"I know you care about other people."

"Look at me, Charlene. Look at me."

She lifted her head, stood in silence, and peered across at the pool behind the twenty-foot horizontal sliding glass door. Her eyes lowered to Amari.

"Please sit down," he said.

She pouted and sulked on the large orange bean bag chair at the entrance to the fitness room and bowling alley.

Amari stood, walked over to her, and sat on the matching footstool. "Charlene, listen to me. My responsibility is to protect my herd of sheep like it's the responsibility for other pastors to protect their congregations. If God has called them to minister, then they know the word of God and have prepared for this day."

"But you said, only God knows the day."

"True. That's why Jesus told us to watch and pray (St. Mark 13:33). There are signs that He told us to recognize (St. Matthew 24:1-44)."

"But everyone is not a minister."

"God has called every man to be a minister; every man must be the leader of his own household because every man has the gift of ministry. It's written, 'As every man hath received the gift, even so minister the same one to another, as good stewards of the manifold grace of God.' (I Peter 4:10)

"Stewards are required to be faithful. How can a faithful man not see the signs of God? How can one who is true in God not see that Donaldson was the devil? And if he was the devil, how can those who continue to walk in his path not be also? But if the blind are leading the blind, where shall they end?"

Her brows lowered.

He held her hands. "If you are not blind, you will not follow the blind. I tell my congregation not to come to church to learn about God, but to fellowship in the truth of God. Learn about God by reading the Scriptures, every man of God has a Bible in his home, so there is no excuse for ignorance."

She pushed forward her bottom lip.

His thumbs were rubbing the back of her hands. "My duty is to my congregation. I'm not Jesus Christ. I cannot save the world. God has appointed me to save the members of the church that He has given for my oversight. Those are the sheep that I'm called to protect.'"

Amari leaned forward with his eyes lifted to hers.

She lowered her eyes to his. "You said you don't love or like me," she whimpered.

"I don't love or like that person that you were allowing yourself to be. There is a person in me that you won't love or like if I allow him to be. We all have multiple personalities. If we do not control them, they will control us. And to control them, we have to know that they exist. These are personalities that surface when you are scared, angry, lonely, insulted, embarrassed, depressed, et cetera.

"I'm letting you know the person that surfaced in you is a woman that I don't like and cannot love. She is not your heart and soul but the natural being of human flesh that is a slave to the things of the world, like fear. God didn't give us the spirit of fear (II Timothy 1:7). I will always tell you what you need to hear, and not what you want to hear."

They locked eyes in silence, and even the children seemed to realize the moment.

"I'm sorry," Charlene murmured.

Amari kissed her.

Yvonne stepped into the walk-in refrigerator and took out a case. "Let's fry some fish."

* * *

The tear gas and bullets didn't deter the daily protesters, who hurled rocks, bottles, and firebombs at the foot soldiers and water gun vehicles in the downtown cities.

Whole families with people as young as nine and as old as ninety were among the millions across the country on the streets in defiance of President Hornsby. To keep those scenes from the eyes of the world, Hornsby tried to shut down the internet, and all communications save XOF and the approved federal government networks. But the underground media continued to broadcast. And when the people learned the new currency trade-in value was only 50 percent, the resistance grew with added defectors from all ranks.

Donaldson's former VP, Peter McDermott, who was secretly leading the resistance, was able to tilt the division in the Pentagon to his side.

The heads at the FCC joined the resistance and broadcast the underground reporter's secret recording of the militia leader, stating that he was given direct orders from Erich Hornsby to kill blacks and Jews.

After the defiant broadcast of that undercover video, the secretary of defense joined the resistance and ordered the

National Guard that was protecting the White House to leave. Some stayed and donned red hats, vowing to fight to the death.

In the other cities, the National Guard and Army Rangers followed the orders to arrest the militia that didn't surrender, and fierce battles erupted in the streets that left many of the residents bagged as casualties of war.

The four-square-mile area had shrunk to two, and the secretary of state, the attorney general, and the head of DHS fled to the White House to stand their ground with Hornsby and the army of forty thousand militia that included mercenaries.

With the attorney general in retreat, the FBI director was empowered to free Hornsby's political enemies and the secretary of defense liberated the internment camps. The Speaker of the House took charge of the presidential duties and addressed the nation.

"Benjamin Franklin was asked, 'Well, Doctor, what we got, a republic or a monarchy?' He replied, 'A republic if we can keep it.'

"I am here to tell you that we have restored our republic. As a little Italian girl, my father told me that when someone calls you a derogatory name, it's because they don't want you to know that name fits them.

"The deep state wasn't on the Left, but on the Right. The FBI has issued a warrant for the arrest of the attorney general, secretary of state, director of DHS, and Vice-President Erich Hornsby. We are restoring law and order to our streets as I speak.

"We are Americans. We are resilient people. No matter how great the evil, we will stand against it and win because we are Americans! We will not lose our republic! We will not become a monarchy!'"

The reporters clapped, and she curbed her smile.

"I have revoked all of the directives given by President Donaldson and Vice-President Hornsby. I will also introduce a bill to reimburse businesses for the damages and losses incurred during martial law.

"Let me close with this: The inauguration for the president-elect, Matthew Mitchell, will proceed as scheduled."

She turned to leave the briefing room and a reporter shouted, "That's ten days away."

She stopped and said, "We will cancel the parade, but the inauguration will proceed with the understanding that the White House will temporarily be unoccupied."

She continued to exit as reporters shouted, "What are you going to do about Erich Hornsby?" "Has Mr. Hornsby surrendered?" "The militia surrounding the White House said they would fight to the death. Are you going to war with them?"

She ignored the questions. The anger she hid in front of the nation was revealed when she entered her office. She immediately phoned the White House. "It's over, Erich. Surrender."

"It's not over. I am fighting to save our country. You are fighting to destroy it."

"Erich, I didn't make this call to debate. I'm praying for you. I'm asking you to spare the country from any more disarray and surrender peacefully."

"I am bringing our country back to the Founders, the Pilgrims, who were Puritans like me. Do you know why they left England?"

He paused, then said, "Because King James was a nigger. You are reading the translation of the Bible that a nigger commissioned. That's why God sent the Puritans to America, so they could build a new England, a country where only white people can rule. What has become of our promised land when a nigger can be president? We are taking our country back from the niggers and Jews and Muslims and faggots that believe they can use the same bathroom as us, drink from the same water fountains, eat at the same table."

The speaker ended her silence, "The Founders wrote that all men are created equal."

"All white men are created equal. Niggers and Jews aren't men; they are animals that look like men."

"Erich, will you surrender?"

He ended the call.

After two days of failed negotiations, the military unleashed its firepower on the ground and in the air, and broke through the militia's last line of defense and entered the gates of the White House.

The team of Navy seals entered the West Wing via the tunnel and discovered Erich Hornsby dead in the Oval Office from a self-inflicted gunshot wound. The attorney general, secretary of state, and director of DHS had also committed suicide in separate rooms.

Arrested and charged with treason were two of the Joint Chiefs of Staff, Hornsby's allies in the Administration and Congress, the known members of the One Percent Leadership Council, and all who had joined the militia. The rogue vigilantes were also arrested and charged with their crimes, but the mercenaries escaped as if they hadn't been there.

America sighed, relieved. But the normalcy the government tried to restore wasn't felt because of the memories and damages left from the civil war. The White House and every building within the four square miles were severely damaged. Many refused to look out the windows of their homes because of the dead bodies that lay in the streets, on their lawns, and on their steps.

But as the much-needed healing for the nation, the inauguration of the president-elect was televised.

On that gray and blustery day, Derrick was sitting at the Capitol's west front in the third row, directly behind where Matthew Mitchell was sworn in. Juna sat to his left, and next to her were Charlene and Amari. At Derrick's right were Yvonne and her husband, Terrance.

Terrance whispered in his wife's ear, "In eight years, you'll be sworn-in as president."

Yvonne whispered back, "Four if Mitchell doesn't stay straight."

After the Church of God and Saints of Christ New Jersey Temple sang "No Turning Back," Derrick whispered in his mother's ear. "We haven't economically empowered every black community, but now we have the financial and political power to do it. Praise God!"

ABOUT THE AUTHOR

Born and raised in Washington, DC, Neal Owens wrote his first story in the fifth grade but didn't consider writing as a profession when he pondered career choices. But after thirty-three of service to at-risk youth, he resigned as the Director of Operations for a nonprofit organization headquartered in the District of Columbia to pursue his passion for writing novels and short stories.

The traditional publishing route was his initial intention, but when he learned that he wouldn't have control over the editing, he decided to self-publish his work.

In following the path of an independent author, Mr. Owens has learned the hardest part isn't finishing the novel but exposing the book to readers. With more than a million books being published each year, it's extremely difficult for an unknown author to become known without a hefty marketing budget or major platform.

As one of the many authors struggling for exposure, his inspiration comes from his wife, Brenda, and children, Joanna, PJ, and Ben-jay, in the knowledge that you are never too old to fulfill a dream. Mr. Owens' favorite shirt says, "I'm Retired, but not Expired."

MIRRORS OF LIFE—Part 2: The Fight for Political Power is the continuation of his debut novel and another gem among the many at the bottom of the tall grass.

www.ingramcontent.com/pod-product-compliance
Lightning Source LLC
Chambersburg PA
CBHW020412080526
44584CB00014B/1287